UNDERSTANDING FAITH

SERIES EDITOR: PROFESSOR FRANK WHALING

Available

Understanding Christianity, Gilleasbuig Macmillan
Understanding Judaism, Jeremy Rosen

Forthcoming

Understanding Buddhism, Perry Schmidt-Leukel
Understanding Hinduism, Frank Whaling

UNDERSTANDING FAITH

SERIES EDITOR: PROFESSOR FRANK WHALING

Understanding Sikhism

W. Owen Cole

DUNEDIN ACADEMIC PRESS

EDINBURGH

Published by
Dunedin Academic Press Ltd
Hudson House
8 Albany Street
Edinburgh EH1 3QB
Scotland

ISBN 10: 1 903765 15 3
ISBN 13: 978 190376515 9
ISSN 1744-5833

BRITISH LIBRARY CATALOGUING IN PUBLICATION DATA
A catalogue record for this book is available from the British Library

Set in 10/12pt Plantin with Stone Sans display
by Makar Publishing Production, Edinburgh
Cover design by Mark Blackadder

Printed and bound in Great Britain by Cpod, Trowbridge, Wiltshire

Printed on paper from sustainable resources

Mixed Sources
Product group from well-managed
forests and other controlled sources
www.fsc.org Cert no. TT-COC-2082
© 1996 Forest Stewardship Council
FSC

For Kishan
born 5 Phagun 535 Nanakshahi Calendar
16 February 2004 Common Era

And we are your children.
Your grace is the source of our countless joys.
No one knows your extent.
Higher than the highest is our Creator.
All existence is perfectly beaded on your thread,
All that happens is by your will.
Your reality, your dimensions, you alone know;
Says Nanak the slave, I offer myself ever to you.

(Guru Arjan, Sukhmani Sahib, Guru Granth Sahib, p. 268)

Contents

List of Illustrations

Preface

My first expression of gratitude must be to Charanjit Kaur AjitSingh, an eminent member of Britain's Sikh community and a kind friend of many years standing. We first met because of our mutual interest in interreligious understanding. She read through the first draft despite being in much discomfort following a knee replacement operation. I am thankful to her for the gentle manner of her comments that have certainly improved the quality of this book.

By coincidence, I too was recovering from surgery during the period of writing. Consequently, I relied even more than usually upon the kindness and help of Gwynneth, my wife, and Eluned, our older daughter, who corrected spellings and grammar – things that spell checkers don't do! More than once, Eluned also brought a wayward computer to a semblance of good behaviour! My friends, especially Professor Hew McLeod, always replied swiftly and helpfully to e-mail requests for guidance.

I must as always thank Sikh friends in Britain and India, America and Australia, for helping me to understand their religion and way of life. Some of them have patiently borne with me for almost thirty years during which time my respect for the Sikh religion has continued to increase. From the Gurus I learned the principle of critical universalism, something that seems to be an important element of many faiths and one worth exploring in this twenty-first century. Attending worship in a gurdwara for the first time, I began to think about activities that I took for granted as an insider in my own place of worship. Studying Sikhism has been an eye-opening and heart-warming experience that I can strongly recommend.

Finally, my thanks to my friend Frank Whaling and to the publishers, especially Anthony Kinahan and my editor, Lucy Byatt, for their patience. Whilst anything good that is found within these pages owes much to the wisdom and guidance of other people, any defects should be regarded as attributable to me alone.

Owen Cole, Chichester, May Day 2004

The Darbar Sahib, Amritsar

Introduction

Religions are sometimes said to have their feet on the ground and their heads in eternity. Accepting this statement as a general guiding principle, my intention in this book is to write about Sikhs, their beliefs and practices and lifestyles rather than Sikhism. I will try to describe and explain what it means to be a Sikh in such a way that should the reader meet one she or he might have some understanding of her or his Sikh humanity, appreciating, however, that although there is undoubtedly a Sikh identity, which is more uniform than that of Christians, who may differ greatly from one another depending on whether they are Quakers or Roman Catholics, African or Dutch, each Sikh is an individual.

The life of an extended Sikh family of Punjabi origin will be the human resource but it will not be followed slavishly, as may be seen, for example, in the chapter on beliefs. It is to be hoped that the reader's next step, if it has not already been made, will take him into a *gurdwara*, where he will find hospitality and friendship and be able to encounter members of the religion at first hand. There can be no better way of discovering and understanding Sikhs than this. Perhaps his journey will eventually be to India and the beautiful and spiritually enriching Harimandir Sahib where our story begins.

First, let me invite readers to consider a conundrum and at the end of the book to offer, should he or she wish, their solution. Neglected, forgotten, ignored, unknown, which of these epithets best applies to Sikhism? The fact of the matter is that it is a religion given little consideration by non-Sikhs. In the UK, for example, since 1968 only four non-Sikhs have graduated at Ph.D. level; it is possible to come across recent graduates who have not had any introduction to Sikhism in their first degree programme and it is rare to hear of possibilities for them to have access to a course lasting more than ten hours. No lectureship solely devoted to Sikh studies exists. Things are better in North America where a place has often been found for the teaching of Sikhism and more affluent communities have funded posts, though these tend to be less traditional. Although most books claiming to be introductions to the world's religions include Sikhism, the media and popular writings often ignore it. Christianity, Judaism, and Islam will naturally be mentioned and probably Hinduism, and perhaps Buddhism, but not Sikhism. One may appear paranoid when reminding gatherings of its existence and asking for it to be included among the monotheistic religions, among which, of course Hinduism should also be listed!

The reason for Sikhism being overlooked might suggest itself to the reader as this examination draws to a close, but I can only offer a few tenuous suggestions. Firstly, Sikhism is an ethnic religion still closely associated with Punjab, culturally, linguistically and ethnically. The vast majority of Sikhs one is likely to meet are Punjabi even though their ancestors may have left the region over a century ago. A change taking place in the Diaspora is a broadening out, but nevertheless the roots remain Punjabi. This may account for some academics ignoring Sikhism unless they have had the good fortune to live among Sikhs in Punjab or in the West. It just has not come to their notice.

Secondly, Hindus usually regard Sikhism to be a form of their dharma and may portray it as such to the wider world. As a minor sect of the great and varied Hindu tradition it is unlikely to be given much attention.

A martial race is how the British conquerors of the Sikh Empire wrote of the community in the nineteenth century. Some observers described Sikh spirituality but many confined their narratives to the history of a valiant people. It was easy to conclude that the Sikhs were a martial Hindu caste rather like the Rajputs.

For whatever reason, Sikhs and Sikhism may pass unnoticed or worse. The first victim of the paranoia following 9/11 was an American Sikh shot at a petrol station. Sikhs have often been taken for Taliban in the USA and during the First Gulf War were considered to be Iraqis.

Instead of pursuing this discussion further, having hopefully impressed the issue upon the reader, we will now turn to our examination of the Sikh faith and the community that exemplifies it.

1

The Darbar Sahib

A Sikh sits at the water's edge looking across the *sarovar* towards the building in front of him, gleaming in the sun. No wonder the British called it the Golden Temple, but the Sikh name is Harimandir Sahib, 'The Divine Temple of God'. Some will use the name Darbar Sahib, 'The Divine Court', but this, strictly speaking, applies to the complex of buildings at the centre of which is the Harimandir Sahib, the most famous *gurdwara* in the world. A photograph of it is to be found in most Sikh homes and there may also be a small model of it standing on a table or shelf.

Our visitor may be resting after an arduous journey or a bare-footed walk on the hot marble pavement that surrounds the sarovar. A lone person will probably be a man; women are usually to be found in the company of their husband or, if a widow, with a brother or son, or other family members. There is no restriction on women entering the precincts alone, but it is customary for them to have other people with them, perhaps other women friends or relatives. For reasons of decorum, they have their own bathing areas on the edge of the sarovar.

Suitable dress is important. Many Sikhs wear traditional Punjabi dress even if they may adopt western fashions at work. When they come to the entrance to the Darbar Sahib they will leave their shoes at the office or with a shopkeeper. Even men who are not Sikhs and may not normally cover their heads will wear a turban or a cloth which passes for one on this occasion. Women may pull a scarf, known as a dupatta, over the head. There should be no bare arms or shoulders. The Punjabi shalwar, a waist-length tunic, has sleeves down to the elbow. Western non-Sikh visitors occasionally cause offence by ignoring the dress code. Sikhs very rarely smoke but, even if they did, they would not do so in the Darbar Sahib precincts or even carry tobacco upon their persons. Alcohol is also forbidden. The visitor or pilgrim will circumambulate the Harimandir Sahib in a clockwise direction, receiving, as Sikhs often say, God's blessing in their right hand. They will usually enter the Darbar Sahib by the main entrance at the Clock Tower. Across the pool they will see the gleaming building.

The Harimandir Sahib is a gurdwara, a place of worship. Strictly speaking, it should not be called a temple because Sikhs do not have an order of priests or rituals that can, in any way, be called sacrificial. Inside, it is a room in which a copy of the sacred scripture, the Guru Granth Sahib, is installed. It is opened at about 3 a.m. daily and not closed until 10 p.m. A relay of readers chants its contents and musicians, known as *ragis*, sing them. The sound is amplified across the sarovar and broadcast by radio stations. Sikhs who sit at the pool edge or in one of the many shaded porticoes may well be meditating upon the words that they hear.

What one sees today is very much the work of Maharaja Ranjit Singh's architects and engineers. He reigned during the first half of the nineteenth century and although the capital of his empire was Lahore, he recognised that the spiritual focus of his faith was in Amritsar. He was responsible for the rectangular geometry of the marble walkway, the parkarma, surrounding the sarovar, and the inlaid marble panels and gold leaf ornamentation of the gurdwara. An inlay of Guru Nanak with his companions Mardana, a Muslim musician, and Bala, a Hindu, at the entrance to the causeway leading to the Harimandir Sahib, bears the inscription which, when translated, reads:

> The wise *Sat Guru* looked upon Maharaja Ranjit Singh, his chief servant and Sikh, and in his benevolence, bestowed on him the privilege of serving the Darbar Sahib.

The Sikhs did not join the independence struggle or mutiny, depending on one's point of view, in 1857, even though the final annexation of Punjab only took place in 1849 and the memory of the conflicts leading up to it was still raw. They had no wish for the restoration of the Mughals. The Harimandir enjoyed British protection and its development was encouraged, even to the extent of a neo-gothic clock tower and steeple being built overlooking it, an out-of-place feature which has since been removed.

The Harimandir may not recall the multireligious nature of the Maharajah's rule – he had Muslim and Hindu advisers and administrators as well as Europeans – but it does remind Sikhs of other occasions and circumstances. Tradition, doubted by some later Sikh historians, tells of the foundation stone being laid by a *Sufi*, Mian Mir, at Guru Arjan's request. The portrayal of Bala, the Hindu, and Mardana, the Muslim disciple, conveys the Sikh message of openness. Hindu mandirs or places of worship have one entrance, facing the rising sun; Guru Arjan's structure had four entrances, making it open

to people of all four castes. Nowadays, Sikhs speak of it being accessible to people from all four corners of the earth.

The history of the Harimandir Sahib has not always been so
felicitous. It was destroyed on a number of occasions by Mughal and
invading Afghan armies in the eighteenth century. Walking around
the parkarma the visitors will come across an inset hexagonal stone
shrine to Baba Deep Singh, one of the most famous shaheeds, or
martyrs, of this period. He died in 1757. Though seventy-five years
old, he was so moved to anger by Afghan sacrilege perpetrated on the
shrine that he came from retirement vowing to cleanse it or die in the
attempt. Some way off his army encountered a larger Afghan force
and in the battle the Baba's head was severed from his body.
According to one tradition, he went on fighting holding his head in his
free hand until he reached the spot that now commemorates the event.
(One wonders whether this is the origin of First World War stories of
decapitated Sikh soldiers continuing to charge forward and reach
Berlin!) Another account says that he continued to lead the advance
but, with death imminent, he hurled his head to where it landed on the
parkarma. Sometimes the two accounts are combined. For the visiting
Sikh today, the spot is a reminder of the strong shaheedi tradition
dating back to the martyrdom of the gurdwara's builder, the fifth
Guru, Arjan, in Lahore in 1606.

Jallianwala Bagh is now a memorial garden site not far from the
Darbar Sahib but not part of the complex. It is, however, a place to
which many visitors to Amritsar go. In 1919, during the *Vaisakhi mela*,
three hundred people died and up to a thousand were wounded, many
of them Sikhs. The British story is that anxious to avoid trouble they
had placed a ban upon public assemblies in the town and that the
people gathered in Jallianwala Bagh were political agitators breaking
the law. Indians tell of a crowd of non-political Punjabis resting during
the heat of the day, waiting to go home as the afternoon became
cooler. Whatever the truth of the different accounts, one thing is
certain, Gurkha troops fired on civilians from the only entrance to the
Bagh. The outcry which followed gave the 'Quit India' independence
movement the rallying cry that was needed; British rule in India was
doomed. Even now British tourists in Amritsar may be warned to
avoid Jallianwala Bagh on Vaisakhi day!

Most recent and controversial of the tragedies attached to the
Darbar Sahib is the storming of it by the Indian army in July 1984.
The repercussions of this event are far from over. For some years
groups of Sikhs had been agitating for an independent homeland,
Khalistan. The militant cause eventually found a leader in Sant Jarnail
Singh Bhindranwale, a religious teacher. He set up his headquarters in

the Akal Takht, seat of Sikh political authority from the time of Guru Hargobind, son of Guru Arjan. A visitor to the Darbar Sahib in 1983 saw blue-uniformed, saffron-turbaned men, armed with automatic rifles, patrolling it. The windows of the Akal Takht were sandbagged. In June 1984 the decision was taken to storm the buildings as it was feared that a mass uprising in Punjab was being planned. Indian army tanks smashed their way along the parkarma, crushing the marble pavement. After a fierce battle Bhindranwale and his followers were defeated; many of them, over five hundred, chose death, martyrdom as they saw it, rather than surrender but one thousand five hundred were captured. The Akal Takht was almost destroyed, though the Harimandir Sahib was scarcely damaged as the two sides treated it with respect. In the fire which engulfed the Akal Takht, however, many priceless artefacts were destroyed, including ancient manuscripts of the Sikh scriptures. The date of 6 June when Bhindranwale died is now remembered in the Sikh calendar as his martyrdom day. On 31 October 1984 Mrs Gandhi, the prime minister who had ordered Operation Blue Star, was assassinated by Sikh members of her bodyguard. In 1988 the Punjab police again entered the Darbar Sahib to arrest militants. This time they chose to make their stand in the Harimandir Sahib itself. Damage done to the building was repaired by a Sikh organisation known as the Guru Nanak Nishkam Sewak Jatha a few years ago.

The Founding of Amritsar and the Harimandir Sahib

Guru Arjan's father, Guru Ram Das, founded the town which eventually came to be called Amritsar, 'the waters of eternal life', from the pool which he began to excavate in which the Harimandir is situated. According to some traditions, the land was given by Emperor Akbar, but this matter is disputed, partly because the Gurus never accepted gifts of this kind. It is also recorded that an existing pool was a place to which pilgrims came to bathe and have their skin diseases, such as leprosy, cured. A jujube tree, Dukh Bhanjani Ber, stands where a crippled man was cured. (He later married Bibi Rajni, a devotee of Guru Ram Das.)

Of the town and pool Guru Arjan wrote:

> This city of my Guru, God, is eternal. Contemplating the Name I have attained bliss and obtained all the fruits that my heart desired. Yes, the Creator himself has established it. I am blessed with gladness and all my kindred and followers are

happy. They all sing the praises of their eternal Lord and all
their affairs are dealt with. Our Lord God is our refuge; our
Father and our Mother. Nanak says: I am a sacrifice to the
True Guru who has blessed the city. (AG 783)

I have seen all places but there is none like you. For you were
established by the Creator, the Lord himself, who blessed you
with glory. Ramdaspur is heavily populated, without parallel,
and of supreme beauty. Whoever bathes in the tank of
Ramdas, his sins are washed away. (AG 1362)

It was, however, Guru Arjan who built the Harimandir Sahib, having
first lined the pool with bricks. The work began in or about 1588 and
was completed in 1604. The Guru helped in the building work and in
the evening when the day's labours were ended, he would sit under
another jujube tree, Lachi Ber, to meditate and plan the next stage.
Overall supervision was entrusted to Bhai Buddha, by then almost a
centenarian, who became a Sikh during Guru Nanak's lifetime. When
the scripture was installed in the newly completed building he was
appointed its first *granthi* or reader. The tree from which he supervised
building operations is called the Ber Baba Buddha. Care has been
taken to avoid the term 'pilgrimage' so far because Sikhism teaches
that members of the *Panth* should not trust in the efficacy of such acts,
which are often dismissed as superstitious. Yet, there is a raised cano-
pied platform on the parkarma called the Ath Sath Tirath where many
visitors bathe either in the hope that they may accomplish the arduous
journey to the sixty-eight Hindu pilgrimage sites around India or,
more acceptably, in the belief that the Ath Sath Tirath has the efficacy
of them all put together. An enclosed, secluded place for women
bathers is nearby.

From this brief description of the Harimandir Sahib and its environs,
and the account of its history some insight into the Sikh psyche might,
hopefully, be gained. It is a subject to which we shall return.

A day at the Darbar Sahib

The daily routine of the Harimandir Sahib has shown little change
from the time of Guru Arjan, though some updating has taken place.
For example, loud speakers amplify the singing of the ragis and these
are also broadcast.

The Harimandir closes for only four hours, from midnight until 4
a.m. Even during this period, volunteer cleaners will be washing the
floors with a mixture of water and milk and drying them with towels,
changing the floor sheets and dusting the walls and panels. The

parkarma too will be washed down. Although the doors to the Darshani Deori, the impressive gateway leading onto the causeway and giving access to the gurdwara, are closed from 11 p.m. until 3 a.m., twenty or thirty singers will chant verses from the scriptures throughout the hours of darkness.

The scripture itself, the Guru Granth Sahib, is carried on a palki, a palanquin, by a group of Sikhs at about 10.30 p.m. Its destination is a room in the Akal Takht, the Kotha Sahib, where it will be laid to rest until 5 a.m. when it will be ceremonially returned to the Harimandir Sahib, accompanied by the beat of large drums, nagara, and chanting Sikhs jostling for opportunities to carry the heavy palki but often eager to encourage visitors to take a turn. Back in its room in the gurdwara, it is installed to the accompaniment of singing and the recitation of *Ardas*, the congregational prayer. A verse will be read from a page opened at random and this constitutes God's *hukam* or command for the day. The magnificent ritual of the Harimandir Sahib is echoed daily to a lesser extent in all gurdwaras where there are officials to perform the duty. Elsewhere it may take place only once or twice a week.

Outside the precincts of the Darbar Sahib, life continues where it had left off a few hours earlier. Stallholders raise their shutters, shuffle their wares around, dust their books and wait for the already arriving visitors. Inside, the parkarma soon becomes hot. Volunteers, sewadars, pour water from the sarovar onto it but this is effective only for a short time. If possible one keeps to the strips and tiles of black marble, which does not get as hot as the white. Water carriers may carry their gifts in buckets, ladling a mouthful into cupped hands.

Langar

Early in the morning langar begins to be served in a special hall which can accommodate about two thousand men and women sitting cross-legged on the floor. This ancient tradition predates the Darbar Sahib, and possibly even the Sikh tradition, for a parallel can be found in Sufi Islam. However, langar has a distinct symbolism. The custom of feeding those who came to receive *darshan*, a grace-bestowing glance from a Guru, began with Guru Nanak. It is unlikely that anyone was ever sent away from his presence hungry. Also the potential devotee would be challenged to accept one of his basic principles, that of eating with everyone else no matter what caste they might have been born into. Commensality is still a major issue in Indian society, and it was even more contentious in Guru Nanak's day.

The classic example of one who would receive the Guru's darshan belongs to the time of the third Guru, Amar Das. The great Emperor

Akbar was the visitor. There was considerable amazement when a person of such eminence was asked to sit on the ground with other men and women and told that he must share langar before he could meet the Guru. He was told: 'Pehle pangat, piche sangat' ('First eat together and then meet together'). Akbar was humble enough to comply with the requirement. The emphasis upon using langar to underline the unity and equality of humankind is attributed to Guru Amar Das. Men and women sit separate from one another at langar for reasons of decorum. The simple vegetarian meal is eaten sitting on the ground. Men and women share in the preparation and distribution of langar, stressing implicitly in doing so the importance of the cardinal ethical principle of *sewa*, voluntary community service. It is probable that the majority of Sikhs who make the journey to the Darbar Sahib will perform sewa in one form or another. It may in the preparation or distribution of langar, or in giving the flour and other ingredients used, or washing the metal plates and other utensils, or scrubbing the floor once everyone has been fed. The Sikhs who give water to those who circumambulate the Harimandir Sahib are performing sewa, as are those engaged in cleaning the parkarma. On arrival at the Darbar Sahib shoes are removed and left in the office or elsewhere for safe keeping. On returning they might have been cleaned: this is the most menial sewa of all but Sikhs may vie with one another to perform it. The many sewaks or sewadars are an ever-present reminder that Sikhism is a community religion and that the worship of God of necessity entails the service of one's fellow human beings.

Kar Sewa

This is an exceptional form of service that used to take place every twenty-five years. Now it occurs more frequently, most recently in 2004. This is a special cleansing of the sarovar which is drained and all the accumulated silt removed by hand in panniers carried by the thousands of women, men and children who come from India and beyond. Those from Punjab arrive in lorry loads early in the day and work until evening, almost without a break. I was present during Vaisakhi 1972 and witnessed the remarkably well-organised activity. The restoration of the Darbar Sahib after Operation Blue Star in 1984 included a special cleansing of the sarovar.

As may be seen from the above brief introduction the Darbar Sahib is a site that evokes many memories in the lives of Sikhs.

The numbering of the plan assumes that the visitor will enter the complex by the main entrance under the Clock Tower, turn left as is the custom, and walk along the parkarma in a clockwise direction until the Darshani Deori is reached and the Harimandir Sahib is

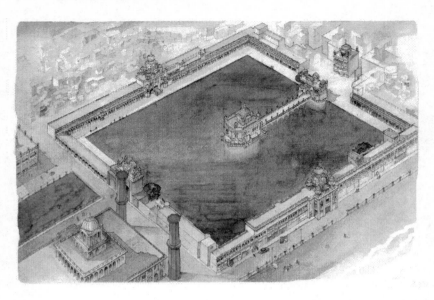

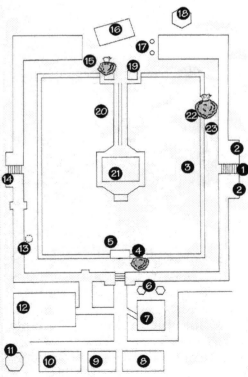

Plan of the Darbar Sahib

1. Main Entrance and Clock Tower
2. Central Sikh Museum
3. Sarovar (Pool)
4. Dukh Bhanjani Ber
5. Ath Sath Tirath (Shrine of the 68 Holy Places)
6. Watch Towers
7. Langar
8. Guru Ram Das Serai
9. Teja Singh Samundri Hall (Management Committee Office)
10. Guru Nanak Serai
11. Baba Atal Tower
12. Manji Sahib Diwan (Asembly Hall)
13. Baba Deep Singh Shrine
14. Entrance and Library
15. Lachi Ber (Guru Arjan Dev's Tree)
16. Akal Takht
17. Flagstaffs
18. Thara Sahib (shrine of Tegh Bahadur)
19. Darshani Deori (Gateway)
20. Causeway
21. Harimandir
22. Ber Baba Buddha (Tree Shrine)
23. Parkarma

approached across the causeway. After paying respects to the Guru Granth Sahib and listening to the ragis, the clockwise journey will continue until the main entrance is reached once more.

2

The Gurdwara and Sikh Worship

Guru Nanak not only taught a distinctive doctrine of personal spiritual liberation, he also established a community. Wherever he preached his followers formed a *sangat*. Its purpose was manifold: to deepen faith and understanding of the message they had received, to live as a community which transcended and rejected caste in its religious life, if not socially, to practise the key social principle of sewa and to worship God through the singing of *kirtan*. These were sacred songs composed by the Guru, and later some of his successors, sung often to the accompaniment of musical instruments, just as the Guru and his companion Mardana, the Muslim musician, had worked together when proclaiming the Word during their travels. An account of their journeys in a *janam sakhi*, a religious biography, often ends with the converts forming a sangat and singing kirtan in a room which may have been set apart for the purpose, a *dharamsala*. It is said that in every house a dharamsala was established. The B40 Janam Sakhi describes the visit of an imperial revenue collector to the place where he was living.

> The karori proceeded on foot and at the place where the Baba's abode came in view he stood and did homage. For three days the Baba detained him and showed much favour towards him. Before leaving, the karori made a request. 'Babaji, if you grant permission I shall build a village in your name and call it Kartarpur. Whatever produce is grown will be contributed to the dharamsala'. The karori then took leave. (pp. 81-2)

Dharamsala nowadays generally describes a hostel and since the days of the sixth Guru places of Sikh worship have been called gurdwaras.

The word gurdwara may mean 'by means of the Guru's grace' (the Guru being God) or 'the door of the Guru'. It may be a room in a house, or the house itself, or a small building in a village, scarcely distinguishable from others but for a flag flying above it. It is used of the magnificent Harimandir Sahib at Amritsar and other famous shrines, and also of one of the multipurpose buildings found in many countries of the Diaspora. One feature determines whether a place is a gurdwara or not, that is the presence of the Guru Granth Sahib, the Sikh script-ure. In fact, for purposes of a particular ceremony – for example, a wedding – a school hall or an open space may become a temporary gurdwara when the scripture is brought to it. Recent guidance from the Akal Takht, however, has suggested that weddings should only be performed in a gurdwara. This has been ignored by many Sikhs, especially as most gurdwaras could not possibly accommodate the families and friends who wish to attend the occasion.

The Guru Granth Sahib must be treated with the utmost respect. The domestic house gurdwara should be a room kept solely for the purpose of housing the book and for worship based on it. The posses-sor should ensure that there is no room above it as this might result in someone passing over it; similarly it should be elevated above floor level so that it, and not other people in the room, provides the focal point. It will be set upon a stool, a *manji*, or on cushions, and a canopy will be set above it, either suspended from the ceiling or part of the manji itself; in such circumstances it is usual for drapes, acting as curtains, to be hung on all four sides. In the early morning after taking a bath, a household member, or even the whole household, will enter the room, head covered and feet bare, bow fully until the head touches the ground.

Every village where Sikhs live will have its gurdwara. This may be only one storey in height and quite small and dark, lit only by oil lamps and with an earth floor. For weddings, the Guru Granth Sahib will be carried from it on someone's head to the place where the marriage is to take place, perhaps a marquee or even the flat roof of a house so that villagers on surrounding rooftops can enjoy a good view of the ceremony.

The Granthi

An official, a granthi, paid a small remuneration, may act as custodian of the gurdwara, opening the scripture in the early morning and closing it at night in ceremonies known as Parkash Karna and Sukhas-san. The most impressive acts of Parkash Karna and Sukhassan may be experienced at about 3 a.m. and 10 p.m. at the Darbar Sahib. It is well worth missing sleep to participate in them. Being a granthi is not a profession in its own right and strictly speaking, anyone may be appointed granthi, and after sometime replaced and expected to return to his former occupation.

The granthi will receive from local families some chapattis and curry to sustain him and feed any persons who may come for langar. This person is usually a man, though in theory a woman could undertake the responsibilities. He will be appointed by the village from one of their members, and his only qualification may be an ability to read the scripture and know the correct way to conduct ceremonies such as naming children or weddings. These are by no means unimportant skills.

Sometimes Sikhs will describe the granthi as their 'priest'. This is extremely misleading and unhelpful. Sikhism is a religion with no priesthood. Within the limits of knowledge and standing in the community, anyone, male or female, may conduct services and ceremonies, though of course only *Khalsa* members can initiate others into that community. (See chapter eleven on initiation.) Christian Quakers or Baptists, for example, have been taken aback and dismayed by this description of a granthi. He should not be regarded as a highly educated person who can answer visitors' questions. His role is simply that of performing ceremonies. Diaspora communities are becoming increasingly aware of the need for granthis to speak the language of the country in which they are resident and to educate the young, but so far the training establishments in Punjab have made little response. There is some debate, especially in the Diaspora, about the need for granthis since everything that they do can be performed by individuals or by the sangat as a community.

Large gurdwaras in towns such as Varanasi or Patiala will be recognisably similar to those found in a house or village. The differences will be in organisation and personnel. For example, there may be a management committee that supervises services, langar, building work, the appointment of professional granthis and ragis, festivities and everything that belongs to its life. Here, the granthi may have been trained at a *gurmat* college providing the kind of education needed by those who take up such appointments. So far, however, this does not seem to include the learning of English, the reason being, it is said, that although one or two students might be engaged by Diaspora communities, most would find employment in India. Women are sometimes educated at such institutions but none has yet been appointed as a granthi; instead they have gone into the teaching profession, often in Khalsa colleges.

Diaspora Worship

Among dispersed Sikh communities in such places as North America, Australasia, and the United Kingdom, the place of the gurdwara is more formalised than in Punjab.

Large gurdwaras may be able to employ one or more granthis on a full-time basis. They will open daily and the routine may be very like

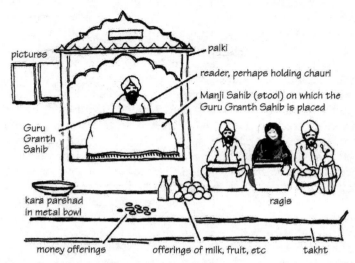

pictures

palki

reader, perhaps holding chauri

Manji Sahib (stool) on which the
Guru Granth Sahib is placed

Guru
Granth
Sahib

kara parshad
in metal bowl

ragis

money offerings

offerings of milk, fruit, etc

takht

(Note: There is no standard or orthodox shape but the
Guru Granth Sahib must always be the clear focal point,
visible from all points of the room.)

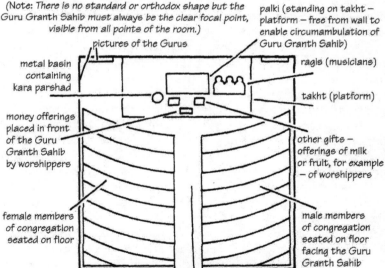

palki (standing on takht –
platform – free from wall to
enable circumambulation of
Guru Granth Sahib)

pictures of the Gurus

metal basin
containing
kara parshad

ragis (musicians)

takht (platform)

money offerings
placed in front
of the Guru
Granth Sahib
by worshippers

other gifts –
offerings of milk
or fruit, for example
– of worshippers

female members
of congregation
seated on floor

male members
of congregation
seated on floor
facing the Guru
Granth Sahib

aisle left free for worshippers to pay their respects to
the Guru Granth Sahib before sitting in the congregation
– sometimes men and women use separate entrances

Sikh congretational worship in a gurdwara.

that in India. Even here, however, most Sikhs will gather at the weekend, especially on Sundays. Though Sikhs do not observe special days, this is the one when most of them will be free from work or school and college. Small communities may not be able to afford to employ a granthi or might regard it as an unnecessary luxury. Members of the sangat well versed in the faith and liturgy will assume responsibility for conducting services.

Sunday worship, *Diwan*, will probably begin and end at set times. At the end of the service *karah parshad* will be distributed, necessary notices given, and langar served. Langar was mentioned in the first chapter but here the binding effect that it has upon the sangat must be stressed. In most, if not all gurdwaras, men and women may be observed helping in its preparation, distribution, and the clearing up that follows. No one should ever refuse to participate in langar since it would be regarded as deeply offensive. Theologically, it might suggest a lack of acceptance of the tenets of the faith. In the Diaspora langar may be eaten at tables or sitting on the floor as in India. There is some dispute between traditionalists, supported by the Shiromani Gurdwara Parbandhak Committee (SGPC), and Sikhs who argue that food is taken sitting at tables in the West and Sikhs should comply. Families will linger over the meal as they may rarely see one another except at the gurdwara – they may well live twenty or more miles from it and the main body of the community. The afternoon may be a time for meetings.

The Diaspora gurdwara serves as a community centre. Features will vary but a major one is likely to be Punjabi classes for the young of the third generation who are becoming increasingly removed from the important culture of Punjab. Learning to read and write the language, something that their parents or grandparents found unnecessary, will be viewed as an important skill. There will also probably be music classes where members can learn the Indian instruments used in Sikh worship and discussion groups where theology and issues facing the Panth or sangat can be examined. Football and hockey clubs, badminton and table tennis evenings can be found. There are Sikh guide and scout troops. Provision for older members is not neglected. They may attend the gurdwara in the evening for prayers, to listen to the activities of the Gurus, and enjoy conversation.

The gurdwara is the focal point of the sangat perhaps to a greater degree than it was in India. What began as a terrace house or old ware-house, converted to serve as a place of worship, is now, very often, a purpose-built complex with many rooms and other facilities, but the most important feature remains the Diwan hall where services are held.

Private or Personal Devotion

Though congregational worship is of paramount importance, Sikhs should also develop a deeply spiritual prayer life. The word meditation might be more suitable but prayer is a word much used by them.

The life of a *gurmukh* Sikh is based on three things: 'Nam japo, kirt karo, wand chako' – namely, practising *Nam simran*, working at an honest calling, and giving in charity. The three are inseparable, but here the emphasis will be on the first. Put together with the other two it is a reminder that Sikhism is a community religion with no room for monastic or ascetic isolation.

Nam japo covers thanksgiving and gratitude for God's graciousness, and concern for oneself and one's family. The Sikh prays: 'manandi himmat baksha', 'Bless us and help us to obey your will'. This does not mean that prayers for one's own needs are unacceptable. As in the *gurbani*, the life of a devotee is a dialogue between the human soul and the Supreme Soul based on grace. What could be more natural than to share one's anxieties with one's closest friend? Seeking to obey God's will prevents prayer from becoming wish fulfilment. It is keeping the mind noble and the heart humble. It is said that

> By obeying God's command, acceptance is gained and one is received in the Divine palace.

There is a sense of awe in the relationship; this is the source of faith and an awareness of unconditional love, but it should never lead to a feeling of such unworthiness that one is reluctant or fearful of praying. This might almost be compared to false modesty.

Hopefully prayer is learned from one's parents, and from one's grandmother in particular. Her absence from many Diaspora homes results in a deprivation that cannot easily be estimated or measured. In Punjab, while both parents are working, the little child observes the grandmother saying prayers and will imitate her. They will go to the gurdwara together to offer mattha thekna, prostration to Babaji. She will tell stories of the Gurus. This is one of the merits of the extended family.

The person praying may use a *mala*, a circle of woollen cords tied in 108 knots. Sometimes it is called a seli. It corresponds in some ways to the mala used by Hindus or Buddhists, Muslims and some Christians, being an aid to concentration, though it is not universally used. As it is passed through the fingers the devotee may utter the word *Waheguru* under the breath. Personal prayer, however, is much more than the repetition of this *mantra*. Sikhs should bathe in the morning at *amrit vela*, between three and six o'clock, the time considered most appropriate for giving the mind to God before the demands of the day take over. The content of the prayers should be the *Japji* of Guru Nanak, the *Jap* composed by Guru Gobind Singh, and his ten swayyas, from Akal Ustad, verses in praise of the Immortal One, sometimes called Invocatory quatrains, Shabad Hazare and the Anand Sahib. At dusk, as day and night come together, Rahiras should be recited or sung. This consists of verses by Guru Nanak, Guru Amar Das, Guru Arjan and Guru Gobind Singh. When sung by a group of young people on a train journey or an individual walking among the trees in a garden it can have a strong effect upon the listener. Before going to bed, when the Guru Granth Sahib is being put to rest, in the gurdwara, or in the late evening at home, the five hymns of Kirtan Sohila are sung or recited. The first three are by Guru Nanak, the fourth by Guru Ram Das and the fifth by Guru Arjan. Its themes are the unity of the human self with the Ultimate Reality, the singularity of the Ultimate despite the endless diversity of scriptures and teachers, and the need to put aside external forms of piety; the believer is finally given a vision of the harmonious worship of the cosmos when loud chanting is replaced by the inner unstruck melody. The unknown mystery is revealed to the person of faith and devotion.

It may be seen from this outline that daily Nam simran is an important way of developing the spiritual life. These compositions are contained, along with other important passages such as Ardas, in a small book known as a *nitnem*, or gutka, meaning Daily Rule. When not in use it will be wrapped in cloth and placed on a shelf above other books. It may be this rather than a copy of the Guru Granth Sahib that most Sikhs will possess.

Prayers at meal times

Sikhs may offer various prayers. Here is one offered before, the other after, the meal. These passages come from the Guru Granth Sahib (pp. 257-9):

> By the grace of the One Supreme Being, the Eternal, the Enlightener:
>
> The Lord is the only giver, who gives to all, without limit, for limitless are his treasures.

> Wonderful Lord, we have partaken and enjoyed the food out of your blessed treasures. We give you many thanks for it. Through Nanak may the glory of your Name increase and may the whole world be blessed by your grace.

3

The Sikh Gurus

Sikhism is not based on devotion to Guru Nanak or any of his successors; a Sikh (Punjabi for 'disciple') is one who is devoted to the spiritually liberating message that they preached. It m helpful here, and significant, to note that the Sikh scri contain little biographical information about any of the (Before long, however, anyone who wishes to understand S must meet the Gurus, in particular the first, Nanak, as Sil some five hundred years ago. What follows is an attempt t out those salient features in their lives and mission that con to an awareness of their roles in the formative era in Sikh life and history from 1469 to 1708, which is known as the Guru period.

The World of Guru Nanak and His Life (1469 – 1539)

Guru Nanak was born in a Punjab village called Talwandi Rai Bhoi, renamed in his honour, much later, Nankana Sahib. It is now in Pakistan. His father, Kalu, was a member of the Bedi sub-caste, or *zat*, of the *Khatri got* (Hindi *jati*); his mother was Tripata. He had one sister, Nanaki, who was some years older than Nanak. The year of his birth was 1469 CE, 1526 Samvat in the Hindu calendar, or year one of the new Nanakshahi Sikh calendar. One tradition gives the precise date as Puran-masi, the full moon day of the month Kattak/Kartik, that is 20 October according to the Gregorian calendar. Another places it on the third day of the light half of the lunar month, Vaisakhi, that is 15 April. Though most scholars favour the latter date, the Kartik tradition is so firmly established in popular religiosity that it is the date celebrated worldwide.

Important Incidents in Guru Nanak's Life

His birth

The traditional sources, known as Janam Sakhis, religiously based biographies, used by Sikhs in their gurdwaras and homes, and providing material for the many 'lives' that may be purchased on bookstalls, describe a wonderful birth and childhood. Brahmin *pandit* and Muslim mullah independently agreed that he would grow up to be an important figure. When it was time for him to be invested with the sacred thread (*janeu*) worn by Hindu men of high caste, ten-year-old Nanak asked whether or not the thread was permanent. When he was told that it had to be renewed annually, he refused to accept it, demanding one that would not wear out! Put to the mullah to study Arabic and the Qur'an, he astonished his teacher who said there was nothing left that he could teach him. His parents saw only a troublesome son and eventually decided to send him to live with his sister who, now married, was living in the town of Sultanpur. Her husband, Jai Ram, was a steward of the Muslim head of the village, Daulat Khan. He secured employment for his young brother-in-law.

His calling to guruship

Early one morning, as was his custom, Nanak went to bathe in the nearby river Bein. He did not return; Daulat Khan ordered an extensive but unsuccessful search to be made. After three days the young man reappeared but remained silent to his family's and his employer's questioning. When he did speak he is credited with the profound but cryptic utterance: 'There is no Hindu and no Muslim, so whose (religious) path shall I follow? I will follow God's path. God is neither Hindu nor Muslim'.

Remarkably this experience is attested to by the Guru Nanak himself in one of his hymns. It is to be found on page 150 of the Guru Granth Sahib and reads:

> I was once a worthless minstrel then the Divine Being gave me work: I received the primal injunction: 'Sing divine glory night and day!' The sovereign called the minstrel to the True Mansion: I was given the robe of honouring and exalting: I tasted the food of the true ambrosial Name. Those who through the Guru feast on the Divine food win eternal joy and peace. Your minstrel spreads your glory by singing your Word. Nanak says, by exalting the Truth we attain the Absolute One.

Few great religious teachers have described their calling in this way. Among Indians there is often a reticence to speak of their spiritual experience. Like a mantra given to a *chela* or disciple by a guru it is unique and not to be disclosed. Guru Nanak, however, was unlike many gurus and presumably wanted his readers to recognise that he was no superman but someone very human whom his followers could emulate. They too could have their 'river Bein' experience.

This is surely the most significant biographical passage in the Guru Granth Sahib.

Soon after this experience Nanak began his mission and must now be called Guru Nanak. Before he set out, however, tradition describes an interesting and provocative interview in Sultanpur with his employer and the village mullah. There was a rumour that Guru Nanak had made disparaging remarks about Islam. He was called to account. The time for prayer came and the two Muslims asked him to pray with them. He did not and, according to one version, he actually laughed as they prayed. Prayers completed, they demanded an explanation. They were told that they were not praying because their intention (niyat), the prerequisite of sincere prayer in Islam, was wrong. The mullah was concerned for his horse standing untethered in the courtyard near an open well, while the nawab had sent a servant to Kabul to sell horses and was wondering whether he had obtained a good price. Neither man's heart or mind was set on God.

Episodes in Guru Nanak's journeys

Tradition affirms that Guru Nanak made five journeys throughout India and into distant lands including Tibet, Sri Lanka, and Arabia, from about 1500 until about 1520. He was usually accompanied by a friend of his youth, from Talwandi, a Muslim named Mardana, a member of a low caste of bards, known as dums or mirasis, and some years his senior. Nanaki, the first person to believe in Nanak's mission, gave him a stringed instrument which he played to accompany the sacred poetic compositions of the Guru.

Talk to most Sikhs, consult almost any biographies of Guru Nanak and such anecdotes as these and those that follow will be told to you. In homes and gurdwaras, they provide the faithful with a portrait of their founder and, perhaps even more importantly, convey some key Sikh teachings.

One night the Guru and Mardana came to the home of Sajjan, the Thug. He had built an edifice which served as a mosque and a mandir. The two travellers were invited to rest in it overnight. It was Sajjan's intention to kill them and rob them as they slept, as was his customary way of treating guests! They sang God's praises into the night and eventually Sajjan was so moved that he came to the place of worship, confessed his evil intentions and wicked life and sought forgiveness. Henceforth the Thug lived a reformed life turning his place of worship into a dharamsala (the name given to gurdwaras until the time of the sixth Guru). Clearly, the significance of the story is to proclaim the power of the *bani*, the Divine Word. It has the ability to reform evildoers and transform them into liberated beings.

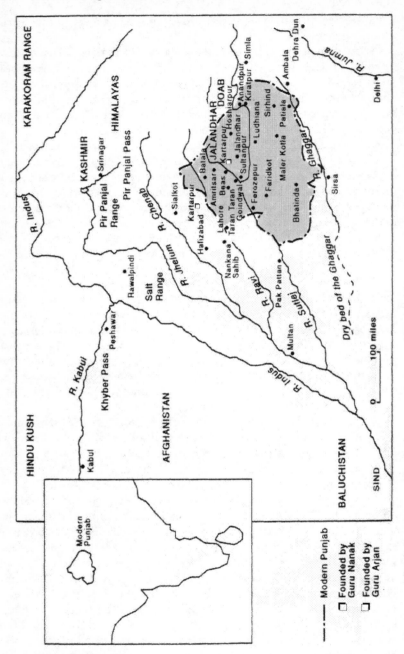

The Sikh Punjab showing some of the main places associated with the
Gurus and the Sikh religion.

Sikhs tell many other stories about the importance of the gurbani, the Guru's Word, not Guru Nanak's but the Sat Guru's, God's. One describes the two travellers as prisoners after the siege of Saidpur with Mardana being forced to hold the reins of a horse. Suddenly, the Guru told him to let the animal go and prepare to accompany the Guru on his rebeck. Mardana protested that the horse might run away and they would be in risk of their lives. Guru Nanak replied: 'I feel the Word descending, play the music!' (The author is not aware of the written source of this story but has heard it often from Sikh friends.)

The choice of Mardana, the Muslim, best illustrates the Guru's attitude to caste and to other religions, but a very popular story is that of Bhai Lalo and Malik Bhago. Guru Nanak went to Saidpur and stayed with the lowly carpenter, Lalo, despite an invitation from the richest man in the village. He, Malik Bhago, gave an annual feast to which the Guru was invited, however he did not attend. Angry and humiliated, the host summoned the Guru to explain his conduct. This he did by taking a piece of the rich man's bread and squeezing it. Out flowed blood! Then he took a piece from Lalo and did the same. Out came pure milk! His bread was earned by honest labour whereas that of the rich man was the product of greed and exploitation.

One of the more amusing stories is of Guru Nanak visiting the village of Duni Chand, another wealthy man. This businessman had the custom of erecting yet another flagpole whenever his fortune increased by 100,000 rupees. He already had many. To teach him the real value of material wealth, Guru Nanak gave Duni Chand a needle, asking him to keep it safe until they met in the hereafter. Pleased to be so trusted by such an eminent man, he ran home to tell his wife, who, instead of sharing his pleasure, scathingly asked him how he would carry it into the next world! Duni Chand realised his folly. Guru Nanak had sharply made his point.

One of the Guru's journeys took him to Hardwar, a north Indian place of pilgrimage. At sunrise a group of Brahmin priests began to make *puja*, throwing water symbolically in the direction of the sun, eastwards. Guru Nanak asked them what they were doing. They replied that they were sending water to their ancestors in heaven. Without a word he began throwing water in a more westerly direction. When they asked him what he was doing, he replied that he was watering his fields in Punjab. If they could send water all the way to the sun surely he could reach Punjab!

Again he encountered a yogi who was exploiting the naïve credulity of a group of villagers by claiming to be able to tell them their future. As he sat, eyes closed in meditation, the Guru took the bowl that lay in front of the yogi and put it behind his back. When the yogi furiously demanded to know who had stolen it, Guru Nanak asked what kind of man claimed to be able to look into the future but could not see behind his back. The falseness of the yogi was brought to the villagers' attention but even more so they were taught that God alone knows and ordains destiny.

An account of the Guru's visit to Makkah (Mecca) is particularly interesting. As usual accounts vary, but they tend to agree on the message that the Guru imparted. Guru Nanak sat with his feet facing the Ka'ba. (If you have done this in a mosque or gurdwara you will know how unacceptable the action is.) The Guru was asked to move his feet and, in one account, he requested the Muslim to move his feet to where the Ka'ba was not. In another as the Guru's feet are shifted so the Ka'ba moves in the same direction! The meaning behind the story is, of course, that there are no sacred places which affirm that God is particularly present there, like the Ka'ba. God is everywhere. The words of Guru Nanak are written on page 84 of the *Adi Granth*:

> Having created the Universe the Creator abides within it.
> The worth of the One who is in the Universe cannot be told.
> In whatever direction I look, in that direction I find God.

On page 433 there is the sentence: 'God pervades everywhere, and alone inhabits every soul'.

One day the Guru arrived at the holy city of Multan where many mystics lived. As he approached a number of townspeople came forward carrying a bowl full of milk to signify that there was no room for further spirituality. Guru Nanak said nothing but took a jasmine flower and placed it on the cream. Then he said that his presence would be no burden but would rather add fragrance to their town!

These stories and many others that can be found in traditional biographies by storytellers, and grandparents, portray a man of humour and insight, of spirituality rather than religiosity, astute, down to earth and impatient with humbug of any kind. These are characteristics found among many Sikhs throughout the history of the Panth, up to the twenty-first century. He scarcely resembles the kindly, white-bearded, other-worldly man depicted in popular, mainly twentieth-century paintings. They also suggest that from the beginning Sikhism, whilst being an emphatically spiritual movement, was one that had strong ethical concerns.

Kartarpur

Finally, Guru Nanak ceased his travels; Mardana was dead and his son had taken his place as instrumentalist and companion. The Guru was not old, about fifty years of age, but he was now not only an itinerant preacher, proclaiming his message to new audiences, he was leader of a community of followers. His task was clearly to provide them with a discipline and, eventually, look to the future after he had gone by appointing a successor.

The traditional accounts of the Guru's life, and those of Bhai Gurdas, relative of the third Guru and an eminent theologian who was born only twenty years after Guru Nanak's death, describe the Kartarpur community in some detail, but more significant may be its presumed effect upon Sikh life five hundred years later.

Amrit vela, the period before dawn, is the time when Sikhs should rise, bath and meditate. This practice probably derives from the example of the Kartarpur Sikhs following the custom of their leader. Honest hard work should be one of the hallmarks of a Sikh; taking alms from no one and following occupations which are of worth to humanity. Some accounts state that the land upon which Kartarpur was raised was given by a wealthy devotee. This assertion is frequently contradicted by Sikhs, as is the allegation that the land upon which the Harimandir Sahib was later built was the result of a similar donation. The Kartarpur Sikhs worked in the fields or as craftsmen with no wish for reward. Sewa, voluntary service on behalf of humanity is a key Sikh principle, perhaps the most important one. Kartarpur is probably the place where sewa began, though it is implied in some of the traditional tales. Sikhs are not the only people to observe the institution of langar, but it is something upon which there is a strong emphasis. In common with other Sikh activities, it was and is a way of binding together the community. Langar, the free meal which is served whenever the gurdwara is open, daily in India, perhaps only on Sundays and at festivals in a country like Britain, where there may be no one available to operate a small gurdwara, is a simple vegetarian meal provided by the community, sometimes by a family on behalf of everyone. Large Diaspora gurdwaras now serve langar daily. All sangat members may participate in its preparation and should share in eating it. It is not a meal to opt into as some are in other faiths, it is something that only the caste-conscious might refuse to share. Any visitor to a gurdwara, regardless of faith, is advised to share in langar to demonstrate human solidarity – and the Indian food is not too spicy, usually. Langar in India is always taken sitting on the ground, outside or in a special langar hall. Since 1998 there has been a dispute in the Panth with the SGPC demanding that Sikhs the world over should follow the custom which, besides being natural in India, was presumably the practice at Kartarpur. Some, perhaps most, Diaspora communities have fallen in line. In Canada at the time of writing the community has been denounced by the SGPC in Amritsar for continuing to use tables and chairs. So something intended to bind Sikhs in unity can be the cause of division! (The story has parallels in other religions, of course.)

The focus of the Sikhs was their Guru. In the evenings after work and probably at other times they could be envisaged gathering in his presence to hear his teaching and sing the bani. The same hymns are still used, just as in the morning a Sikh should recite the Japji, the one composition that has not been attached to a musical raga and is placed at the opening of the Adi Granth. This, of course, is what Sikhs do today, except that the Guru Granth Sahib contains the compositions of five other Gurus besides Nanak and bani by non-Sikhs like Kabir. Here a question poses itself. Who assembled the words of these men? It is known that they were in use when the fifth Guru came to compile the Adi Granth. In all probability they were first of all collected by Guru Nanak on his journeys. Of all the Gurus he was the man who would possess the authority to introduce them into the community's worship. More work needs to be done on this matter before this suggestion wins total approval, though many scholars now accept it.

Shared lifestyle, shared food, shared work and shared worship with a shared loyalty to the Guru must have welded the Kartarpur community into something vital and created an ideal up to which the Panth has not been completely able to live in later times. One thing remained for Guru Nanak to do: it was necessary to provide a successor. History is littered with idealistic groups who fade away once the founder has gone.

Guru Nanak saw the need all too clearly. Three candidates are traditionally listed. Two were his sons, which indicates that some, if not all, of his family were members of the Panth. The third was a disciple named Lehna, another Khatri who converted to Sikhism during the Kartarpur period, probably when he was in his twenties. Bhai Gurdas presents the overall situation very tersely:

> Baba Nanak then proceeded to Kartarpur and put aside all the garments of a traveller. ['*Udasi*', the word employed here can mean renunciant or traveller. Some translators have opted for the first interpretation, but it seems that he was indicating that his missionary journeys were largely at an end. He had entered a new phase in his life.] He clad himself in ordinary clothes, ascended his gaddi and thus preached dharma to his people. He reversed the normal order by, before his death, appointing the disciple Angad as Guru and bowing before him, for his sons did not obey him, becoming instead perfidious rebels and deserters. He gave utterance to

words of Divine Wisdom, bringing light and driving away
darkness. He imparted understanding through discourses
and discussions, the unstruck music of devotional ecstasy
resounded endlessly. Sodar and Arti were sung in the evening
and in the morning the Japji was recited. Those who followed
him cast away the burden of the Atharva Veda [and put their
trust in the Guru's hymns]. (Var 1)

The Atharva Veda is the fourth Veda. Part of it consists of spells
for averting physical troubles and the like. Sikhs should have no
truck with superstitious practices, as these would be called. The
verse is mainly spiritual in content. Two main points emerge. First,
the utter spirituality of life at Kartarpur, and second, the threat from
his sons. The elder of the Guru's two sons, Shri Chand, was a pious
man but an ascetic. He was not the person to lead a community
founded on the basis of living a normal householder existence. His
brother, Lakshmi Das, seems to have been indifferent to the religious
life and probably had no inclination to be considered for guruship. A
janam sakhi account tells of the Guru's attempt to find a suitable
successor. A water pot lay in a muddy ditch; he asked his sons to
recover it. Shri Chand refused because he would be polluted. The
other son refused to demean himself, this was no job for a Guru's
son. A Sikh named Lehna jumped into the ditch without being asked
and not only retrieved the lota but cleaned it and gave it to the Guru
filled with clean water. In this way the Guru showed the Panth who
should succeed him. He renamed the disciple Angad, which means
limb, one of his limbs, so close was the relationship. To prevent any
uncertainty and dispute he then actually installed Angad as Guru
and became his chela.

During the Kartarpur period the Guru also travelled locally. Not
far from the village was a dera or camp of Siddhas, and it may be
these whom he visited, though the encounter could have taken place
elsewhere and earlier. Siddhas or Naths, the Janam Sakhis use the
terms interchangeably, believed that by the practice of yoga they
could acquire supernatural powers. They were feared by villagers,
much as they are today. This antisocial attitude plus their apparent
belief that they could manipulate God and gain liberation by their
austerities, which made them superior to God, having a hold on the
Divine Being, made the followers of Gorakhnath, based at Achal
Batala not far from Kartarpur, a group not to be tolerated. Their
practices and teachings flew directly in the face of the man who
proclaimed liberation through the householder life of being married
and working hard with honesty. The full discourse, presented in the

form of a debate or discussion is to be found on pages 937 to 946 in the printed versions of the Guru Granth Sahib.

Death of Guru Nanak.

There are two main traditions relating to the date of Guru Nanak's death. The Puratan Janam Sakhis give the date as Asu Sudi 10, 1595, in the light half of the month. According to the Gregorian calendar, this would be sometime in September 1538. The Bala Janam Sakhis offer Asu Vadi 10, the dark side of the month Asu, that is 15 days earlier than the Gyan-ratanavali date, and the year 1596. Scholars like McLeod seem prepared to accept the Asu Vadi 10 date, 7 September 1539, but cannot be said to give it whole-hearted support (McLeod, 1968, p. 101). We might then be correct in saying that Guru Nanak was born on 15 April 1469 and died on 22 September 1539.

All accounts agree that the Guru died at Kartarpur and few people argue with this. The best-known story of his death tells of an argument between his Hindu followers and those who came from a Muslim background. Doubtless in some dismay, that his teaching about the efficacy of one form of disposing the body over another had eluded his disciples, he ordained that he should be placed on the ground, his corpse covered with a sheet and that in the morning they would know what it was proper for them to do. Some accounts state that he instructed them to put flowers on either side. In the morning when they returned it is said that both collections of flowers were blooming but the body had disappeared. Thus neither cremation nor inhumation was sanctioned – or, on the contrary one can argue that both were acceptable. As a matter of fact, it is the Hindu tradition of cremation that has been adopted by the Panth, though in Muslim countries inhumation is acceptable unless the family wishes to take the body to India. Presumably the reason for cremation is that followers from Hindu backgrounds have always predominated in the Panth. There is also a belief that the Guru went, in his body, to Sach Khand, a heavenly abode to which the spirit goes at death. There, he confirmed to his disciples his vision of the unity of the community.

Social issues were of considerable concern to the Guru. In this respect Sikhism might be described as a very worldly religion, that is one that takes the world seriously rather than dismissing it as irrelevant to the attainment of spiritual liberation. There were some members from Muslim communities but most were of Hindu background, most seem to have been Khatris many from low-caste groups, not many were Brahmins.

Guru Angad (born 1504, Guru 1539–1552)

When Guru Nanak asked someone to retrieve a water pot from a dirty
ditch the man who obeyed him was Lehna (also known as Lahina).
Another, more gruesome story, is also told about him. One day Guru
Nanak took his followers into the wilderness. As if by magic gold and
silver coins appeared, many Sikhs ran around gathering them up.
Those who had not done so went further with the Guru and just as the
money had materialised so did precious jewels which attracted all but
Lehna and another Sikh. Guru Nanak led them to a funeral pyre on
which lay a shrouded corpse. He asked them to remove the shroud
and eat the body! The other Sikh fled, leaving only Lehna who
prepared to do his master's bidding. On removing the cloth, he found
not a dead body but Guru Nanak. The incident had been instigated by
the Guru to test his disciples. One meaning of the episodes of the
water pot and funeral pyre may be to deny the concept of ritual pollution, but it is chiefly to affirm the loyalty and obedience of Lehna
whom Guru Nanak initiated into guruship soon afterwards. It is not
unusual for spiritual leaders, just like secular ones, to appoint successors. Guru Nanak's reasons for doing so were probably his awareness
of the need for someone to guide the young Panth and his realisation
that neither of his sons was suitable to fulfil the role of Guru. Shri
Chand did become a guru, founding the Udasi Panth, but his celibate
ascetic way of life did not fit him for leadership of a movement that
emphasised the householder lifestyle.

Guru Angad became a Sikh sometime after Guru Nanak settled at
Kartarpur. He was a Khatri of the Trehan got, from the village of
Matta di Sarai, in the Ferozepur district, who, on his marriage to
Khivi, the daughter of a Khatri, moved to her village of Khadur where
he became priest of the temple of Durga. He met the Guru with a
group of villagers and decided to join him in Kartarpur. He and his
family moved to be with him. He is said to have been born in 1504,
but neither the date of his conversion nor that of his installation is
known. He became Guru on the death of the first Master in 1539 and
died in 1552.

Lehna was named Angad by Guru Nanak as something of a pun on
the Punjabi word ang, meaning 'limb'. He was saying that Guru
Angad was his limb. One of his first acts when he became leader of the
Panth was to move to Khadur where he established his *gaddi*.
Presumably this was to remove himself from the rivalry of Nanak's
sons and to provide himself with his own spiritual base. Although the
Panth was in no sense a political movement and would not be until the
next century, it would have already possessed some wealth in the form

of land and donations and might have been a prize for envious claimants

Guru Angad is commonly believed to have invented the script used to record the compositions of Guru Nanak, which later became the script of written Punjabi. There was, however, an alphabet already used by Khatri traders, and it is most likely that the second Guru formalised it. The name of the script is *gurmukhi*, meaning 'from the Guru's mouth' because of its association with the compositions of Guru Nanak and his successors. His role was that of a consolidator of Guru Nanak's work. He composed sixty-two *shloks*, couplets. The Panth continued to be a religious movement, open to men and women of all groups, religious and social. Its composition had not changed since Kartarpur days.

Guru Amar Das (born 1479, Guru 1552–1574)

His home was the village of Basarke, near the site of the later town of Amritsar. It is said that he was on his way to the Ganges, at the suggestion of another follower of Vishnu, when he heard his nephew's wife, Bibi Amro, the daughter of Guru Angad, singing one of Guru Nanak's compositions. This prompted him to go to Khadur instead of the sacred river. There he became a Sikh. The significance of this story is that it illustrates the impact of the sung Word rather than the voice of the singer, however mellifluous it may have been.

The two sons of the second Guru are said to have been unsuited to leading the Panth, consequently he turned to his devout son-in-law. The Guru instructed him to settle in the village of Goindval, a few miles from Khadur, from which he walked every day to bring Angad water for bathing. It is also the place where he established his gaddi when he became Guru at the age of seventy-three. One of the reasons for this must have been the potential threat from rivals who included Shri Chand, Guru Nanak's surviving son.

At some time during his guruship Guru Amar Das decided to construct a steep stepped well. It is still in use today and attracts many Sikh visitors. Its purpose is not to provide water for drinking or irrigation but for ritual ablutions. The width of each step must be over five metres, a metal rail runs down the centre so that women and men may descend separately. The large circular pool at the bottom is probably about one and a half metres deep and about eight metres in circumference. The presence of such a well is significant in itself, but perhaps more notable is the fact that it has eighty-four steps, corresponding to the number of lakhs (a hundred thousand) of rebirths that a Hindu might have to undergo if he finds no other way of abbreviating the cycle of rebirth necessary to achieve spiritual liberation. Pilgrims to the baoli sahib as it is called, the sacred well, tell of the belief that whosoever recites Guru Nanak's Japji eighty-four times will be liberated from the cycle of rebirth.

Guru Amar Das appointed twenty-two manjis, women and men, whose primary function was to preach and teach the practice of Nam simran. This decision is indicative of the expansion of the still young movement and the consequent need to respond to the proliferation of sangats. In addition, some women, known as peerahs, were appointed to preach among women, Muslims in particular.

Sikhs were also instructed to assemble wherever the Guru happened to be at the Hindu spring festival of Vaisakhi (or Baisakhi) and, in the autumn, at Diwali. The Panth was still concentrated largely in Punjab and the Guru saw these occasions as opportunities to emphasise and strengthen its coherence and focus leadership upon himself. His summons presented Sikhs with a choice, to assemble in his presence or continue to celebrate the Hindu festivals in which they had been nurtured.

The appointment of manjis and peerahs may be taken as a sign that the still young Panth was expanding steadily, and possibly spectacularly, in the area where Punjabi was the major regional language. The assemblies were intended to wean Sikhs away from major Hindu events, possibly challenging them to decide which of the two paths they would follow. At first, the baoli sahib seems contrary to the teachings of Guru Nanak that pilgrimage and bathing at *tiraths* to remove ritual pollution, in which he did not believe, were futile. It must be explained in terms of the third Guru's recognition that there were already people joining the Panth who did not necessarily share the beliefs of its founder in the essential inwardness of spirituality, the realisation of liberation through Nam simran and not outward religious forms. Even though Guru Nanak's death lay only a generation in the past or less, and there were many of his early followers still living, it was necessary to adjust to the changing circumstances that Guru Amar Das faced. That he did so is a sign of wisdom.

Langar has already been mentioned in chapter one. This was a practice that Guru Amar Das emphasised strongly. Akbar's visit must have greatly affected Sikh morale as is emphasised by the fact that pictures on the walls of gurdwaras often depict Akbar cross-legged in the midst of lines of people of obviously lesser status.

Guru Amar Das's insistence on langar may indicate a Panth in danger of forgetting the teaching of Guru Nanak. Class-consciousness exists in the Sikh community today. An ideal society may have existed at Kartarpur, but at Goindval what is known as a process of institutionalisation may have begun. Members of its community might have been attracted by a variety of factors which may or may not have included a deep and fervent faith in the teachings and principles of the founder, especially in a culture that emphasised, and still does, corporate allegiances rather than the pursuit of individual aspirations and ideas. This is something that westerners may find difficult to appreciate and understand while Sikhs may not like to admit such developments. Evidence of factional rivalry among Guru Nanak's sons who aspired to guruship, however, indicates lapses from the idealism of the early Kartarpur community.

Important in the bani of Guru Amar Das is his opposition to the practice of sati, the custom of a widow immolating herself on her husband's funeral pyre. In adopting this stance he was following the precepts of Guru Nanak who opposed the seclusion of women, dowries, and female infanticide, common practices in Punjab of his time. Guru Amar Das wrote:

> Do not call her a sati who burns herself on her husband's body. Know her to be a sati who dies from separation from God. (AG 787)

The persistence of critical allusions to these social ills, as the Gurus saw them, indicates that they were far from eradicated from the practices of Sikhs. Members of the Panth may be reluctant to admit this, but it is a fact of life among most organisations, political as well as religious.

Guru Ram Das (born 1534, Guru 1574–1581)

Named Jetha by his family, he was the son-in-law of Guru Amar Das. He was nominated by the third Guru and on his accession took the name Ram Das, slave of God. He established a number of towns, the most important one being Ramdaspur, later known as Amritsar. Town building may have been designed to provide the Panth with greater focus and cohesion as well as assisting the mercantile interests of his many Khatri followers, but Amritsar came to have an added purpose, perhaps from its inception. Guru ka Chak, the Guru's village, was a place to which Guru Ram Das, and some Sikhs say, Guru Nanak, went to meditate, in a hut by a pool known as the pool of nectar. From this came 'Amrit' in the title of the town, meaning nectar, and 'sar', from sarovar meaning pool. Tradition asserts that he excavated the existing pool to create the large expanse of water that may be seen today.

Guru Ram Das also created a system of delegated authority. Instead of the manjis of his predecessor, he appointed a number of masands (a form of the Arabic 'masnad', one who sits on a throne) to share in organising the Panth and to be responsible for the collection of tithes which they brought to the Guru at the festival gatherings. They were appointed by the Guru himself and responsible directly to him. The system worked well at first but eventually the masands became corrupt, seeking to establish their own authority and use the money for their own purposes. They survived, their power steadily growing until the tenth Guru, Gobind Singh, abolished them.

Guru Arjan (born April 1563, Guru 1581–1606)

The fifth Guru, the first to have been born a Sikh, found himself at the head of a steadily growing Panth that could attract the attention of a Mughal Emperor, owned land, and extended throughout Punjab and beyond. Less than fifty years after Guru Nanak's death it might be regarded as a successful, if mainly regional, movement.

Guru Arjan inherited the usual situation of insecurity in the form of his elder brother Prithi Chand whose challenge persisted into the life of the sixth Guru. In 1618 the pretender died, but his followers, who came to be known as minas, 'dissemblers', among other members of the Panth, caused trouble throughout much of the seventeenth century, even preventing the ninth Guru from entering the Harimandir Sahib, which they controlled.

Guru Arjan, second son of Guru Ram Das, is known for two things: first, his construction of the Ram Das Sarovar, the pool where bathers may remove all ills and impurities, and the building of the Harimandir Sahib, a physical focus for Sikh spirituality. As we have seen already, it is the place that all Sikhs aspire to visit even though pilgrimage is not considered an acceptable activity as it puts the emphasis upon outward, ritual conduct rather than inward behaviour. Nevertheless, work on the building went on steadily in conformity to a peculiarly Sikh design. Hindu mandirs have one entrance at the top of a flight of steps facing the direction of sunrise. The Harimandir was rectangular with an entrance in each side; each entrance was approached by descending steps, on the principle that anyone coming into God's presence must become as humble as possible. Guru Arjan also wrote:

> The four castes of Kshatriya, Brahmins, Shudras and Vaish-yas are equal partners in divine instruction. (AG 747)

Access to God should not be restricted.

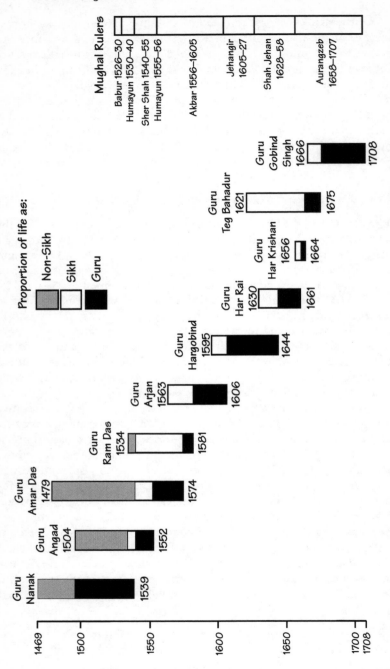

The Sikh Gurus in their Mughal context.

Second, in 1604 the Guru's other great work was completed: the compilation of the Adi Granth, the Sikh scripture. The account of the progress of Sikhism to becoming a religion of the Book will be considered later, but this must be seen as the greatest achievement of the fifth Guru's life.

This year may well have marked the apogee of Sikhism. It enjoyed a focal point, a scripture, and the ear and interest of the liberal-minded Emperor Akbar the Great. Perhaps the Guru hoped that the message he represented might become the one to unite the Mughal Empire. Reasons for this view lie in the emperor's inclination to welcome men of various faiths to his court, for example Jesuits who hoped that he might convert to Christianity, a thought which filled orthodox Muslim courtiers with apprehension, and Sufis such as Mian Mir who respected Sikh teachings. Some traditions even suggest that he laid the foundation stone of the Harimandir Sahib. Scholarly opinion disagrees with this suggestion but it does accept that he and the Guru knew and respected one another. It is also affirms that Akbar showed an interest in the teachings expressed in the Adi Granth.

Disaster

Scarcely had the Adi Granth been installed than the emperor died. The usual war of succession took place and the Guru was implicated. Some scholars accept the view that the Guru blessed one of the claimants, Khusrau, as he passed through Punjab, but most deny that its purpose was to support his cause. The successful son of Akbar, Jehangir, had no such doubts. He ordered the arrest of Guru Arjan who was brought in chains to Lahore for interrogation. Accounts of his death in 1606 differ, but Sikhs agree that he died as a martyr, faithful to the teachings of Guru Nanak. Mian Mir is said to have wished to plead for his life but the Guru forbade him. A large fine was imposed on the Panth and the young Guru Hargobind, Arjan's only son, was imprisoned while the community collected his ransom.

Three major events have affected the Sikh psyche, the first and most devastating of which was the martyrdom of the fifth Guru. Relations between the Panth and the civil authority which had seemed so auspicious became based upon a distrust from which they never recovered. The other two events were the martyrdom of his grandson, the ninth Guru, and the assault upon the Darbar Sahib in 1984. Anyone who wishes to understand Sikhism should be aware of the impact of these events.

Guru Hargobind (born 1595, Guru 1606–1644)

Hargobind was born at a time when his father may have been giving up hope and thinking anxiously of the threat that Prithi Chand would present when a successor had to be chosen. The Guru's relief and joy at his son's birth, can be summed up in his own words:

> The Sat Guru has sent the child. The long-lived child has been born by destiny.
>
> When he came and acquired an abode in the womb his mother's heart became very glad. The son, the saint of the world-ruler (Gobind) was born. The primal writ has become manifest among all.
>
> In the tenth month by the divine command (hukam), the baby has been born.
>
> Sorrow has left and great joy become manifest. The Sikhs sing the gurbani in their joy. (AG 396)

Eleven years later the child became Guru and a prisoner in Gwalior Fort until the fine imposed on the Panth was paid. He wore two swords, one of *miri*, symbolising the kind of authority associated with a temporal ruler, someone like the Mughal Emperor, the second representing *piri*, spiritual authority. Miri-piri became part of the concept of guruship from that time. He also wore an aigrette in his turban.

Relations with Jehangir improved once the Guru had been released. They went on hunting expeditions together. His assumption of a regal lifestyle is said to have aroused the critical interest of Goswami Ram Das, guru of the great nationalist Sivaji who said: 'I hear that you are the successor of Guru Nanak. Guru Nanak renounced the world; you wear a sword, keep horses and an army and are addressed as Sacha Padshah. What kind of a sadhu are you?' The Guru replied that saintliness was within, sovereignty was external. Sacha Padshah, 'True King', was a term used by Guru Nanak to describe God, but from the time of Guru Hargobind it was used increasingly to refer to the Sikh Gurus. It was also used by Mughal rulers.

Bhai Gurdas was a relative of the Guru, and served successive Gurus from the time of his kinsman, Amar Das. He was the first Sikh historian and theologian, and the amanuensis chosen by Guru Arjan to compile the Adi Granth, though there is a story that none of his own compositions was allowed to be included as he was already sufficiently conceited! In one of his poems he expressed the ambivalence of some Sikhs towards Hargobind:

Formerly the Gurus used to sit in the dharamsala.

The present Guru does not stay in any one place.

Emperors called at the residences of former Gurus.

The present Guru was imprisoned by an emperor.

Formerly disciples could not find room in the over-crowded congregations,

The present Guru roves around fearing no one.

Former Gurus gave consolation sitting on a manji,

The present one keeps dogs and hunts. The former Gurus would compose hymns, listen to them and would sing. The present Guru does not compose, listen or sing. His companions are not Sikhs, he has wicked and bad people as his guides.

He continues:

Yet the truth cannot be concealed, the Sikhs are enamoured of his lotus feet like bees. He supports an intolerable burden without complaint. (Var 26)

Facing the Harimandir Sahib, the focus of piri, housing as it does the scripture, stands the Akal Takht, the Throne of the Timeless One, the principal centre of temporal authority in the Sikh religion. It was built by Guru Hargobind to symbolise and actualise the doctrine of miri. It marks a distinctive development in the life of the Panth, one that was to be completed in 1699 when Guru Gobind Singh founded the Khalsa.

Two further aspects of Guru Hargobind's reign might be mentioned as they affect the lives of the Sikh community. First, the above passage from Bhai Gurdas uses the word dharamsala. This was the original name given to a Sikh place of worship; now it is known as a gurdwara. One cannot say with certainty that the sixth Guru coined the expression but it becomes the accepted term from the period of his guruship. Second, on the road from Chandigarh to Anandpur Sahib one passes through the small town of Kiratpur founded by the Guru. There his ashes were placed in the nearby river Sutlej. One can often see devotees standing on a small jetty continuing the practice. The remains of some Diaspora Sikhs are also taken there.

The sixth Guru was the first not to compose a bani that is included in the Adi Granth.

In this introductory study whose purpose is to enable the reader to understand Sikhs and their beliefs and practices, it is almost unnecessary to mention the seventh and eighth Gurus, Har Rai (born 1630, Guru 1644–61) and Har Krishan (born 1656, Guru 1661–64) when he died in Delhi of smallpox. Sikhs consider all Gurus to have been equally inspired each filled with the divine *jot*. Touching stories of the child Guru attending to the needs of smallpox victims until he himself succumbed are to be found in books for children and, not surprisingly many schools, dispensaries and other social and charitable institutions bear his name.

The importance of scripture will be dealt with in detail elsewhere but one incident concerning Guru Har Rai's son, Ram Rai, might be told in this section. Emperor Aurangzeb became suspicious of Sikh loyalty being informed that the Adi Granth contained anti-Islamic material. The Guru was ordered to present himself at the royal court to defend himself. He sent his fourteen-year-old son, Ram Rai, instead. Ram Rai prevaricated, explaining the offending text as a scribal error. When the Guru heard of this he denounced his son, informing him that he would never be allowed to look on his face again. Ram Rai remained for the rest of his life at the royal court. The story is a popular way of communicating the teaching that the word of scripture is sacrosanct.

Guru Tegh Bahadur, born 1621, Guru 1664–1675

The surviving son of Guru Hargobind had fame thrust upon him. Designated Guru by his predecessor, his time in office coincided with that of Emperor Aurangzeb who was a zealot in the cause of Islam. Mandirs were demolished and mosques built in their place. The degree to which he persecuted non-Muslims is disputed. Certainly, he eagerly advanced Sunni Islam.

According to Sikh tradition, a group of Hindu Brahmins from Kashmir sought darshan of the Guru at his home in Makhoval, a village near Kiratpur, now the large town of Anandpur, asking him to shield them from the conversion attempts of the emperor. He agreed and offered to ask for a personal audience with the emperor. Muslim accounts assert that the Guru was travelling around Punjab and beyond collecting money and soldiers to lead a revolt. The Guru was ordered to appear before the emperor to answer the charges that were levelled against him and was faced with the choice of conversion or execution, unless he could perform some amazing miracle. When he refused to acquiesce he was executed in Delhi at a place now marked by the Gurdwara Sis Ganj in Chandi Chok. His son, the future Guru Gobind Singh, who is said to have encouraged him to take up the Brahmins' cause, later wrote:

For their [the Brahmins] frontal mark and their sacred thread
he wrought a great deed in the Age of Darkness.

This he did for the sake of the pious, silently giving his
head.

For the cause of truth he performed this deed, giving his
head in obedience to his resolve.

Bogus tricks are for counterfeit conjurors, deceits which
God's people must spurn.

Dashing himself on the ruler of Delhi, he departed for
God's abode. (Guru Gobind Singh, Bachitar Natak, translated by Hew McLeod)

When Bachitar Natak was composed is uncertain, but it appears to be
an early endorsement of the tradition current among Sikhs.

There were followers of the Guru in the crowd, witnessing the
spectacle of his execution; none of them came forward to collect his
body. At night a group of Sikhs, sweepers of the Ranghreta clan or got,
took it. They reached the place where Lakkhi Shah and his son lived
with their companions, the men who had risked their lives to smuggle
away his headless body. As they were being pursued by Mughal
soldiers, they decided to cremate the body using their own house as a
funeral pyre, now marked by the site of Gurdwara Rekab Ganj. Meanwhile, Bhai Jaita and his companions took the Guru's head, wrapped
in a cloth, to Makhoval where his son cremated it, but not before he
assured the Ranghretas that their courageous deed and loyalty would
always be remembered. Jaita was later initiated into the Khalsa,
assuming the name Jivan Singh; he died at the battle of Chamkaur in
1704.

Guru Tegh Bahadur's sacrifice and martyrdom is seen to be an act
of great heroism in the cause of inter-religious harmony. He did not
die for Sikhs but for Hindus and, through them, for all persecuted
minorities. The anniversary of his death is celebrated with multifaith
gatherings and *nagar kirtan* processions.

Guru Gobind Singh (born 1666, Guru 1675–1708)

Sikh homes normally have a picture of Guru Nanak in their main
room. Should they have a second it will be of Guru Gobind Singh.
The contrast in the representation of the two men could not be
greater; the first Guru is depicted as a kindly, white-bearded elderly
person, the last is a warrior, youthful, armed, with a plumed turban,

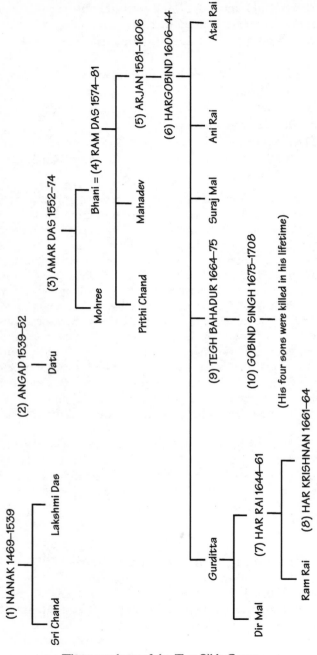

The genealogy of the Ten Sikh Gurus.

and seated on a fine charger. The images are not really accurate in their message. As we have seen Guru Nanak could be stern, a person of authority; the tenth Guru could be compassionate as well as brave: for example, when he forgave and reaccepted into service forty men who had deserted from his army during the siege of Anandpur.

Guru Gobind Singh's given name was Gobind Das or sometimes said to be Gobind Rai, but from the founding of the Khalsa he is known as Guru Gobind Singh.

In 1699, at the festival of Baisakhi, he summoned his Sikhs to come to him armed at Anandpur, the town formerly known as Makhoval. The place is marked by the historic gurdwara Anandpur Sahib. There, in their presence, he performed a remarkable, symbolic act. Sword in hand, he asked whether there was a Sikh present who would give his life for his Guru. Eventually one of his followers came forward and was led into the Guru's tent. When Gobind Das reappeared he was alone, his sword dripping blood. He asked for the head of another Sikh and after some delay one came forward. This happened a further three times, with some Sikhs leaving bewildered and in panic. He then brought out all five Sikhs, unharmed and wearing an identical uniform. The Guru spoke to the assembly telling them that he needed men who would loyally follow him, even to death. The five underwent a rite of initiation, he himself became the sixth member. The ceremony included the sprinkling of *amrit*, a liquid made from water and sugar crystals provided by his wife. Many men became members of what he said was the Khalsa on that day. Khalsa was a term used by Mughal rulers to refer to property that was exclusively their own. Members of the Sikh Khalsa promised obedience to the Guru alone.

What actually happened to the five men, the Panj Piare, was not disclosed by the Guru. Conjecture abounds but is best avoided. What really matters is the Guru's reason for his action. His purpose in founding the Khalsa has been much debated. One reason can be ruled out immediately, the desire for revenge against Emperor Aurangzeb. Twenty-four years had elapsed since the Mughal ruler had executed his father. The emphasis on personal allegiance suggests that this was a way of winning authority back from the masands, who, in fact, were summarily dismissed and removed from office. Much of the Guru's reign was taken up in fighting against local rulers and the Mughals. The creation of the Khalsa as a loyal and quasi-regular fighting force may be another reason. The original five initiates, the Beloved Five, or Panj Piare, came from different social groups. All of them now took the name Singh, the name of Rajput warriors, meaning lion. Women may not have been initiated into the Khalsa until many years later, but female members of Khalsa families would take the name Kaur, usually explained as princess – Sahib Devan, the Guru's third wife, came to be known as Mata Sahib Kaur, the Mother of the Khalsa. Sikh names will be discussed elsewhere but here it must be pointed out that by adopting the names Singh and Kaur, members were effectively declaring that the names by which their social group could be recognised were irrelevant and unacceptable among Sikhs who had sworn loyalty to the Guru. Understanding the Khalsa ideal is essential for a real comprehension of Sikhs and their lives.

Much of the Guru's lifetime, especially after 1699, was spent fighting. In fact a verse attributed to him reads:

> Grant me this boon from your bounty, O God. May I never refrain from righteous acts. May I fight every foe in life's battles without fear and claim the victory with confidence and courage. May my greatest ambition be to sing your praises and may your glory be engrained in my mind. When this mortal life reaches its end may I die fighting with unlimited courage. (Chandi Charitra, Swayya 231)

Sikh relations with the Mughals varied from time to time during the lifetime of the tenth Guru. After Aurangzeb, Bahadur Shah became emperor. In 1708 the Guru agreed to accompany him on an expedition to the south. He was assassinated at Nander but before dying of his wounds was able to instruct his followers that, instead of another human Guru becoming his successor, guruship should pass to the scripture. Thus the Adi Granth became known as the Guru Granth Sahib. The reason for this decision is uncertain, but during his lifetime he had lost all his four sons at the hands of his enemies and there was no obvious spiritual and military leader to take his place. A struggle for the Guru's gaddi might have ensued. As a result of this decision, the Guru Granth Sahib assumes a transformed significance, becoming the focus of corporate and individual Sikh life. During the troubles of the eighteenth century, decisions were made by consulting the scripture which accompanied the Sikhs into battle.

The fundamental teaching about the human Gurus is expressed in Bhai Gurdas' words:

> During his lifetime he installed Lahina as his successor, and set the Guru's canopy over his head. Merging his light in Guru Nanak's light, the Sat Guru changed his form. None could comprehend this mystery; he revealed a wonder of wonders! Changing his body he made Guru Angad's body his own. (Var 1, Pauri 45)

The light or jot illuminating them all was the same; their spiritual teaching did not change. Thus the scripture does not assign a particular bani to Guru Nanak, Guru Arjan, or Guru Tegh Bahadur, but Mahala 1 (or M1), Mahala 5 (M5) or Mahala 9 (M9). The word's meaning is uncertain: mahal can mean 'place' as in the Taj Mahal, and it may also be interpreted as 'the abode of the Eternal Being', *Akal Purukh*. However, its significance is clear.

The apparent difference between the leadership of Guru Nanak, for example, and Guru Amar Das who devised a place of pilgrimage, the Goindval baoli, and the festival assemblies, or Guru Hargobind who kept an army and concerned some of the Panth by behaving unlike his predecessors, may be explained by changing and developing circumstances, such as the Sikh movement attracting the interest and suspicion of an emperor. Had Guru Hargobind lived in the days of Guru Nanak, they might say, his policy and style of leadership would have been very different, but it is not a question that Sikhs normally consider appropriate for discussion.

4

God in Sikh Teachings

It is the teaching of Gurus not their persons that constitute the essence of Sikhism. Frequently, they described themselves using the epithet *das*, servant or slave, or as messengers. It was the message which gave liberation, not devotion to the Gurus.

According to Indian religious traditions the ill which besets humanity is ignorance. True reality, the real purpose of life and the nature of our being, is hidden by materialism. The story is told of a Brahmin, a member of what might be considered the spiritual elite from which priests and pandits come; only they have the right to learn and teach the sacred Vedic texts. This particular Brahmin used his privilege greedily. Not God but gold was the focus of his life. He hid the cash he received for his ministrations in a hole in the river bank, in case anyone should break into his house, and during the night he would go and count it. When he died he was reborn as a water rat so that he could be near his wealth. Water rats have no use for gold, and he quickly learned that the focus of his life as a Brahmin had been wrong. When he died he was restored as a Brahmin. Remembering his lesson, he followed the spiritual path for which he was intended and at death attained liberation, becoming one with ultimate Reality, Brahman.

The Sikh Gurus' vocation may be said to have had only one purpose, to prevent people, both men and, unusually for India, women, from going the way of the materialistic Brahmin, and help them reach their spiritual destiny. They did this by preaching and teaching meditation, awareness of and response to God, so enabling them to achieve spiritual liberation. To say that they aimed to enable people themselves to have the experience which Guru Nanak enjoyed at Sultanpur is not to suggest that their teachings lacked coherence or that they had no theology. On the contrary, their thinking was clear and consistent. The finest detailed study of Guru Nanak's thought may be that of Professor Hew McLeod (*Guru Nanak and the Sikh Religion*, 1968, pp. 148-226). At the beginning of his analysis he writes:

The fact that Guru Nanak's thought is not set out systematically does not mean that it was necessarily inconsistent. On the contrary, one of the great merits of his thought is its very consistency. (p. 149)

It was because of the practical nature of his mission that his teaching was not systematic; he was no armchair theologian but a man driven by the never dimming vision which he received when 'taken to God's court' while he was living at Sultanpur. It does, however, mean that the ideas and terminology which he uses cannot easily be isolated one from another as will be seen from many of the quotations contained in the following pages. The principal source of quotations will be Guru Nanak's compositions. The message of his successors has yet to receive such exhaustive treatment. We will begin by examining the concept of God.

God in the Teachings of the Gurus

The first point that must be made is that they were monotheists and the Sikh religion, consequently, is fiercely monotheistic. It is necessary to stress this as a commonly held view, at least in the West, seems to be that only Islam, Judaism and Christianity fall into this category. Anything emanating from India is most likely to be dubbed polytheistic. This is not true of the essence of Hinduism; it is certainly a false analysis of Sikhism. These are some examples of what Guru Nanak said:

> The One is contained amongst all. (AG 931)
>
> The spouse is but one. All other beings are God's brides. (AG 933)

Many such passages exist, too many to quote. The Japji alone contains a large number of them. Often the affirmation is accompanied by the denial that there is any other being:

> I am ever a sacrifice to you. In the whole world there is but the one True One. There is no other. He alone performs service [sewa] on whom God casts a gracious glance. O my beloved, how can I live without you? There is no second, my love, to whom I may go to utter praise [or of whom may I speak]? (AG 636)
>
> There are six systems, six their teachers [gurus], and six their doctrines, but the Guru of gurus is the One, though having

various vestures. Follow the system in which the praises of the Creator are sung. (AG 356; the word Guru is often used as a synonym for God)

Sikhs frequently call God Waheguru, meaning literally 'praise to the Guru', or 'the wonderful, awe-inspiring Guru'. Guru Nanak used the names Akal Purukh, the Being Beyond Time, but also the honorific title Sahib, meaning Lord, Ram, Hari, from Hinduism, and Allah or *Khuda* (Creator) from Islam. On page 64 of the Guru Granth Sahib there is a list of Islamic names for God: 'Allah, Alakh, Agam, Kadur, Karanhar, Karim.' Man Mohan Singh translates the passage as: 'He is the unseen, inscrutable, inaccessible, omnipotent and bounteous creator.' Clearly, sectarian names meant little to Guru Nanak. In preaching to Hindus he would use names with which they were familiar, if his audience were Muslim he would respect their sensibilities by using Islamic terms. The message mattered more than engaging in wrangling which would only deflect his hearers from listening to and accepting the truth which he was eager to convey. Sectarian argument would defeat his purpose completely. As he once said: 'Without the Guru one prates, prattles and wrangles' (AG 466). The Guru's last word on the subject of the oneness of God is

Your names are countless. I do not know their end, but I am sure that there is no one else like you. (AG 877)

The names given to God may be unimportant but there is no suggestion that God becomes incarnate in any form as some Hindu teachings assert. The use of the name Ram or Hari, for example, did not imply the acceptance of the Hindu mythology associated with them. Guru Nanak and Guru Gobind, in particular, describe themselves as divinely appointed messengers sent by God to alleviate the sufferings of humanity in the so-called Kal Yug, Age of Darkness, when God's teachings are forgotten, but they never described themselves as incarnations.

God is also the Creator:

God is unseen, inscrutable, inaccessible, omnipotent, and is the bounteous Creator. The entire world is subject to coming and going. The merciful One alone is permanent. Call that One permanent whose head does not bear the writ of destiny. ... Day and the sun shall depart, night and moon shall vanish, thousands of stars shall disappear. The One alone is eternal, Nanak speaks the truth. (AG 71)

Of creation he says, in a long passage quoted only in part here:

For countless ages there was utter darkness. There was no earth or sky. The infinite One's will [hukam] alone pervaded. There was neither day nor night, moon nor sun, but the One sat alone in profound meditation.

He goes on to assert that there was no caste, whether Brahmin or Khatri (it will be remembered that the Gurus were Khatris), and no religious dress, no rulers or subjects, no mullahs, no pilgrimage to Makkah, no friends or family, no Vedas or Qu'ran.

When God so willed God created the world and without support sustained the firmament ...The One created Brahma, Vishnu and Shiva, and also maya [delusion].... God created the creation by the divine hukam and watches over it. (AG 1039)

The implication is that where God is perceived and the hukam obeyed all other things or beings will be seen to be *maya*, false, and unreal. Only the One will remain for the spiritually aware. So the Guru could say:

Wherever I look I find the One. (AG 357, where it occurs twice)

The One gives, the One takes away. I have not heard of another, a second. (AG 433)

From the formless, nirmula, God became nirguna, without attributes, and saguna, with attributes or qualities. (AG 940)

The Being Beyond Time, Akal Purukh, without attributes, seemingly paradoxically assumes attributes which in Hindu teaching are often of a material and physical nature. The avatars, incarnations of Vishnu, are God as *saguna*. Sikhism, however, rejects any belief in anthropomorphism. As we shall see, it does believe that God is the initiator of spiritual enlightenment and liberation. For this to be possible, the One cannot remain ineffable but must be self-revealing. It is this that Guru Nanak had in mind when he described God as both *nirguna* and saguna. Lest anyone might still argue that God, as saguna Brahman, becomes an avatar, Guru Nanak made many statements which contradict the belief. God is self-creating (AG 932) and immanent, 'contained amongst all' but 'manifested only to those who receive divine grace'. Further in the hymn, the Guru declares

Self-creating the One is responsible for installing the soul in the body. God is beyond comprehension and humans are involved in worldly affairs. The life of the world shows the way to union with the One.

Guru Arjan said: 'Cursed be those lips that say that God takes human form!'(AG 1136)

The Creator, Kartar Purukh, is within creation but discernible only to those who have been granted divine revelation. Meritorious deeds and other forms of religiosity are vain. As Guru Nanak said in the Japji:

> Good actions may procure a better form of life, but liberation comes only through grace. (AG 2)

> Creating creatures, the One places itself within them. The Creator is detached and limitless. No one knows the mystery of the Creator. What the Creator does surely comes to pass. (AG 937)

This may be described as panentheism. This is the belief that everything exists within God who is immanent throughout the universe, though greater than it. It is certainly not pantheism, the belief that God is within all life, which is the complete opposite. This, however, is not so much a doctrine as an experience. It may be significant that the above quotation comes from Siddh Gosht, the Guru's discussion with a group of yogis who stressed detachment. Nanak is saying that God is the only being who is really detached and that this detachment, unlike theirs, carries with it involvement. God is active without being subject to karma, something which the yogis, by their conduct, hoped to avoid.

> The wise and beauteous Purukh is neither a woman nor a man, nor a bird. (AG 1010)

As Creator God was responsible not only for nature, including humanity, 'creating the whole world with ease', but also the Vedas (AG 930). 'God is the life of the world, besides whom there is no other' (AG 931).

In some respects Nanak and his successors were not utterly persuasive, after all devotees wanted a human personality whom they could trust and in whom they could find support, comfort and consolation. Bhai Gurdas wrote, a century after Guru Nanak's lifetime:

> Hearing the cry of humanity the Beneficent One sent Guru Nanak into the world. Although Guru he performed the humble service of foot washing and provided nectar for his own disciples to drink. In this Age of Darkness he revealed

that there is One Supreme God ...Baba Nanak ferried the
Age across the ocean of existence by proclaiming the mantra
of the True Name. (Var 1, Pauri 23)

Though he accepts that Guru Nanak was God's humble servant,
nevertheless he asserts that his birth was non-karmic. In other words
his entry into the world was the consequence of Akal Purukh's desire
to send a messenger and not the result of conduct in a previous existence as is the case with most, if not all, human beings. The belief that
the other human Gurus were sent into the world predestined to be
God's messengers is a common Sikh belief. It comes close to the
Hindu doctrine of avatar, the belief that God becomes incarnate for
the purpose of delivering humanity from some evil threat. Guru Arjan
declared:

May that tongue burn by which it is said that God, who neither
comes nor departs from this earth, becomes incarnate. The God of
Nanak is all-absorbing and ever-present. (AG 1136)

Characteristics of God

Love is one of the main attributes of God:

By grace the love and affection of God is attained. Without
God who has obtained peace? (AG 937)

Its fruit is peace, sukh, the opposite of dukh, sorrow or pain: 'With
your soul, body and mouth, utter Nam constantly and virtue and
composure will enter your mind.'

This leads to freedom from the burden of desire for material goods
and other anxieties: 'Whoever realises the One deems alike poison and
nectar' (AG 937).

Another consequence of love is the removal of fear and doubt:

The Guru's servants are pleasing to God. They are forgiven
and fear of death is removed. (AG 1190)

Fear may be the most pervasive of human characteristics, especially
fear of death but also a host of other anxieties. The Guru recognises
this, and finds a remedy in fearing God – a state of awe may be a
preferable word:

Fear of God is very great and very heavy. Man's intellect and
speech is paltry. Walk placing God's fear on your head and
bear its weight. The one on whom the gracious glance of the
Merciful falls, through the Guru meditates on God. Without
God's fear none can cross the world-ocean. Fear and dread of

God bedecks man's love. The body's fire of fear is burnt away
by dread of God. With God's fear and fright man's speech is
fashioned and decorated. What is fashioned without God's
fear is utterly worthless. (AG 151)

God is dynamic

In some forms of Hinduism Brahman, Ultimate Reality, is aloof from
the world and the ideal is to achieve a similar detachment. Guru
Nanak's God is dynamic and so must be his followers, hence the principle of sewa, the service of humanity.

God is contained in all created beings. Having created them
they have been put to work. Those who receive grace take
Nam. Putting creatures to work God has made maya sweet to
them. God gives food and drink. Whatever befalls people, the
divine will and command [hukam] should be endured with
equanimity. Parmeshur, the One who created the world,
beholds it. God, all pervading, inside and out, tastes and sees
everything. Why quarrel, mortal? Meditate and be absorbed
and sacrifice yourself to the True One. There is no other giver
than the One who, creating all creatures, gives them sustenance. (AG 434)

In this quotation, God is seen to be the vital cause of human effort.
There is a suggestion of predestination as the Divine Hukam, order or
command, is the cause of all that befalls humanity and the rest of
creation. The omnipotence and sovereignty of God are brought out
clearly in the following verses.

By the Divine Will [hukam] all forms were created; what that
Will is, no one can say. By that Will, all life is formed and, by
that Will, all life is exalted. The Will determines what is high
and what is low; the Will grants all joy and suffering. Some are
blessed by the Will, others migrate from birth to birth. All are
within the Will, none stands apart. Says Nanak, by recognis-
ing the Will, we silence our ego. [The last word in Punjabi is
haumai which Manmohan Singh renders as 'pride']. (AG 1)

Predestination, if that is what underlies much of the Guru's teaching,
is not a judgement of eternal damnation. Following the way of maya,
false reality, results in death. It is a path chosen by the individual.
There are signposts to mukti, liberation, if people will heed them.
There is an element of judgement in Nanak's bani, but death and

transmigration, the ultimate penalties, are the consequences of following maya and one's own ego (haumai).

> The One, who cannot be called to account, issues the true orders and warrants. Nanak says, seeking and searching your own home obtain Nam. Purukh is omnipresent, immaculate and omniscient, administering justice and merging beings in the knowledge of the Guru. (AG 1039)

> If one is full of sins and prays, he is pardoned. By the Guru's grace the evil intellect is eradicated. (AG 357)

God is the sustainer of life

Sometimes God has been compared to a watchmaker who, having made the universe and set it in motion, does not interfere further in its working. The idea can be modified to include miracles and events like the incarnation of a divine messenger, their role being to repair the watch or ensure that it keeps time accurately. Guru Nanak rejects any ideas which conflict with a belief in God as permanently active in creation. In particular, he had no place for the Hindu concept of avatar, divine incarnation. Sikhs may accept that Rama and Krishna may have been heroic human beings who were apotheosised by their supporters. Miracles are also unacceptable; even though some are recorded in the Janam Sakhis, they too seem to suggest that God is not in control of events. The only miracle was that of God's Word.

> God is the creator, omnipotent and bounteous, who gives sustenance to all beings... There is no abiding place other than the One. (ASG 474)

Earlier on page 474 these words occur: 'Meditate constantly on the Lord by serving whom solace is attained.'

God is also beneficent; this is a frequent statement. A passage from the Japji will suffice to illustrate the point:

> The Giver gives, the receivers tire of receiving; age upon age they eat and eat the gifts. All are directed by that Will; says Nanak, the Carefree is ever in bliss. (AG 1)

It may therefore come as a surprise to find God described as the Destroyer: 'The One who builds all, demolishes all as well. Besides God there is not another' (AG 934). But the purpose of destruction is renewal:

Having destroyed, God recreates and having recreated, destroys. God destroys at will. Rebuilding and having rebuilt God demolishes. God filled the sea and then caused it to dry up. The One who alone is beyond all care and dependence has the power to do this. (AG 935)

In the monotheism of Guru Nanak, there is no place for a Shaitan, Satan, the Devil, or any other evil power. God as the only actor must be responsible for every facet of life and experience. While it is a fact that Guru Nanak talked about the destructive activity of God, it is equally clear that the primary work of God, the Creator, is to help humanity realise its union with the One and this is done through the *Shabad*, the Guru and the Hukam, which are studied below.

Let me grasp this one thing: all creatures have one Provider, may I not forget this. (AG 2)

God is sovereign

As sovereign, God's writ or command is supreme:

God's writ is over all beings. There is none who is exempt from it. God is without a writ, creating the creation God beholds it, and causes the hukam to be executed. (AG 598)

Mortals do such deeds as the Creator ordains. They seek to do no other acts. (AG 581)

The initiative and the achievement are completely and solely ordained by God. In a verse not wholly lacking in humour, or perhaps irony and sarcasm, the Guru may have had the yogis whom he criticised so frequently in mind when he said:

I may make a cavern in a mountain of gold or in the waters of the nether world. I may remain standing on my head, upside down, in the earth or on the sky. I may cover my body and wash my clothes daily. I may shout aloud the white, red, yellow, and black Vedas. Or I may live in dirt and filth... Judgement is in the True Guru's hands. What the Creator does comes to pass. It cannot be effaced by human attempts to erase it. (AG 139)

In this section on the Sikh concept of God most of the ideas and terms which will be discussed in subsequent pages have been introduced. As with most accounts of human need and divine response, the key to understanding lies in the meaning of the Timeless Divine Being, Akal Purukh.

5

The Human Condition

We are now in a position to discuss teachings focusing on human liberation. They were addressed as warnings to people such as Sajjan, Duni Chand and Malik Bhago, but doubtless Bhai Lalo and even Akbar were encouraged by them in their determination to centre their lives on God. These ideas will be approached by examining three questions which compare humanity to a patient in urgent need of treatment. Guru Nanak may be seen as a physician. His mission, as stated in his account of the river Bein experience, was to spread God's glory by singing God's Word, and thereby exalting the Truth, so helping his hearers to be aware of, and realise in their lives, unity with the Absolute Being, Akal Purukh (AG 150). This was also the function of each of his successors.

The British Open University offered a course originally titled 'Man's Religious Quest'. It covered many life stances and religions besides asking questions of a philosophical nature. The approach chosen for the study of religions was to ask three questions relating to salvation/liberation: from what? to what? by what means? Stated in terms of a patient suffering from an illness, the process might be expressed in the following way. The first question was, 'What was the malady from which humanity was suffering?' The second question was, 'What should be the state or condition of the cured person?' And finally, 'How, or by what means, could the cure be effected? What was the remedy?'

Original ignorance (avidya) may be said to be the besetting issue of Indian spirituality. It is not any more pardonable than the plea of someone in a law court. 'Ignorance is no excuse in law' they will be told. Guru Nanak taught that the One God created the universe and decided that the means of its development should be by making male and female forms, but this apparent duality was to be seen as unreal, a delusion. Human beings should be able to look through it and beyond it to spiritual liberation. However, the natural condition of human beings, according to Guru Nanak, is to be *manmukh*.

Manmukh

The person who is deluded and self-centred, ruled by self-delusion and ego, is said to be manmukh, one who is dominated by the needs of self. A literal translation is 'one whose face is turned towards her/his own '*man*'. (The term is placed within inverted commas to distinguish it from the name given in the English language to male human beings!) An adequate translation of 'man' into English is difficult. Among the terms offered by Professor Shackle are mind, intelligence, understanding, heart, soul, psyche, the heart as centre of false passions, the false self, ego. McLeod agrees with Shackle's definitions but describes it as 'heart, mind and soul'. He also points out that it is the one indestructible attribute which must be released from the body and merged into the being of God. He distinguishes between the 'man' of unregenerate humanity, to use a term he uses frequently, which leads one into worldly attachments that are the 'very antithesis of salvation', and the 'man' which has become God-centred. On the one hand

> The 'man' is a priceless pearl; dwelling on the Name it has been accorded honour. (AG 22)

But also

> The 'man' is unsteady, it does not know the way. One who puts his trust in his own 'man' is as one befouled; it does not recognise the Word. (AG 415)

So Guru Nanak can say:

> The 'man' of the mammon worshipper is a mad elephant. It wanders about distracted in the forest of delusion. Under the pressure of death it goes here and there. Searching earnestly it will find its home through the Guru. Without the Guru's Word [shabad], the 'man' finds no place of rest. Remember God's pure name and relinquish haumai. (AG 415)

The manmukh may be intentionally self-oriented or it may be an almost accidental condition. For example, the proper affection that all parents have for their children, not only those who are described as 'doting', can result in the spiritual dimension of life being forgotten. Whatever the reason, its consequences are the disasters of death and rebirth. The manmukh is subject to delusion and self-centredness. The last sentence quoted above conveys some of the idea of how the condition of the manmukh may be treated, but first it is necessary to consider further the terms which the Gurus used, maya and haumai

Maya

Human beings are victims of delusion or maya. In the Hindu philoso-
phy of Advaita Vedanta, maya is unreal, an illusion. This is not the
meaning of the word when used by the Sikh Gurus. Maya is real,
though impermanent, hence the preference for the term 'delusion'. It
refers to false values and that which is not true. Above all, it replaces
the unity of life with the idea of duality. Guru Nanak lists a number of
things which constitute maya:

> Love of gold, silver, women, horses, couches, sweets, food,
> and the delights of the human body; how can God's Name
> secure a place in lives filled with these? (AG 15)

A few lines further on he describes 'man intoxicated by the pill of falsehood', which enables him to forget death and make merry for four
days. Real intoxication is enjoyed by those who enter God's mansion
and taste the wine of Truth, which is prepared without drugs. Maya is
compared to a foolish bride who, enjoying her husband's love, prefers
to satisfy her pride elsewhere:

> O silly woman, why are you proud? Why do you not enjoy
> God's love in your own home? [i.e. in your inner being]. The
> bridegroom is near, O foolish bride. What are you looking for
> as you look abroad? (AG 722)

Maya and the remedy for it occur in the same passage. The Guru not
only warned his hearers of the consequences of maya, restlessness and
instability – one of his favourite criticisms – he offered them the way of
avoiding its disastrous consequences. It is actually latent within them,
if they but knew and perceived it. This is well brought out in the
following verse composed by the third Guru. Guru Amar Das wrote a
verse that illustrates the devastating effect of serving the self ('man'):

> When it pleases God a child is born and the family is well
> pleased. Love of God departs, greed attaches to the child and
> the writ of maya begins to run. God is forgotten, maya wells
> up and one is attached to the love of another. Says Nanak,
> those who enshrine love for God, by the Guru's grace obtain
> the Divine in the midst of maya. (AG 921)

Duality has maddened man's mind. He has wasted his life in
greed. Duality has clung to mortals and no one has over-
whelmed it. Implanting Nam within, the True Guru [Sat
Guru] saves man from it. Neither is the mind overpowered,
nor does maya [love of mammon] die. The One who has

created all this alone understands the mystery. Meditating on the Guru's Word one is ferried across the dreadful world-ocean. Amassing wealth [maya], kings become proud. Wealth [maya] does not go with the mortal at death. The love of maya, is of many kinds. Without Nam no one is man's friend and comrade. As is a man's own mind [man], so he sees the mind of another. As is a man's desire so his state of mind becomes. As is one's deeds so is he attuned. Seeking the True Guru's [Sat Guru] advice man finds the place of peace. Singing and hearing secular music, man's mind [man] is attached to duality. Within him is deceit and he suffers great pain. Meeting with the Sat Guru he is blessed with right understanding and remains merged in the love of the True Name [Sach Nam]. (AG 1342)

Maya is variously translated as mammon or greed in the above passage, but it is more than the acquiring or seeking of material possessions. It is untruth as opposed to Truth. In another sentence it is expressed thus: 'The false worshipper of mammon does not like the truth so, bound to duality, he comes and goes. No one can erase what is written', but then Nanak continues: 'Through the Guru one is liberated (AG 109).

Again the diagnosis is accompanied by the cure. Professor Shackle notes the word maya as being used 135 times by Guru Nanak and provides the following meanings: 'the world and its snares, worldly delights (apparently real, but actually corrupting), one who follows worldly goals, intoxicated with worldly delights, being captivated by the world, entranced with worldly delights.' Some of the qualities listed above may seem unexceptionable. Their fault lies in making people self-dependent or independent, that is, forgetful of God. To be good, even if it is possible, is not enough. Liberation lies in being focused on and trusting only of God and obeying the divine hukam (command or order).

The 'man' in itself, however, should not be regarded as evil, but only when it is dominated by selfishness.

Haumai

At the particular or individual human level the main affliction which ignorance results in is haumai. Sometimes it is said that the term comes from two words, meaning I and mine. It is often translated as self-centredness. Haumai, however, is more than an attitude, it is a condition from which human beings in their unenlightened state suffer.

In a long passage in which the hearer is warned against haumai, and ego and self-centredness (which Man Mohan Singh translates as pride) are denounced, the Guru says:

> In pride one comes and in pride one departs. In pride one is born and in pride one dies. In pride one gives and in pride one takes. In pride one earns and in pride one loses. In pride one becomes true or false. In pride one reflects on virtue or vice. In pride one falls to hell or rises to heaven. In pride one laughs, in pride one weeps. In pride one is soiled and in pride washed clean. In pride one loses caste and kind. In pride one is ignorant and in pride one is wise. One does not know the way of liberation and salvation. Maya is pride and one is overshadowed by pride; if self-centredness [haumai] is stilled, God's door is found. Without divine knowledge man prates, prattles, and wrangles. Nanak, by God's command [hukam], destiny is recorded. As man sees God so he becomes aware of haumai. (AG 466)

The effects of haumai are clear. There is no hope for one who is in a state of haumai. A decent ethical life, by temporal standards, may be possible but it is purposeless in an ultimate or eternal sense. Coming and going, transmigration, is the inevitable consequence, though, as usual, the remedy is offered; here it is described as obedience to God's order, hukam, a word which we shall come across later.

> Led astray by doubt, men become crazy. What can be obtained without good fortune? (AG 935)

The Gurus often speak of five evils, passions or impulses. These are kam (lust), krodh (anger), lobh (covetousness), moh (attachment to worldly things – the fruits of maya), and hankar (pride or arrogance). They are all consequences of haumai. In the following verses their effect is outlined, even if not all are specifically mentioned:

> Night is the summer crop in the field of lust [kam], and day is the winter crop in the field of wrath [krodh]. Avarice is the time for the tenant and the ploughman to sow worldly love. Thought is the plough and evil the corn heap. This is what one earns and eats according to God's will. When he is called to account, his life and that of the parents who bore him go in vain. Make fear of God the farm, purity the water, truth and contentment the bullocks, humility the plough, the mind the tiller, meditation the proper condition of the soil, and union

with God the suitable time. Make God's name your seed and God's grace your corn heap. Thus the whole world shall seem false to you. Nanak, if the merciful one shows mercy, then your separation will come to an end. (AG 955)

Wherever there is desire there is destruction and ruin and the bowl of duality and selfishness bursts. Nanak prays, I am a slave to one who remains detached amid the snares of worldly attachment. (AG 840)

Because of haumai many have died and have rued doing evil. The one who recognises God's command, utters God's praise and becomes glorified with Nam through singing the Gurshabad. Everyone's account goes to God's Court; one is exonerated through the beauteous Nam. (AG 109)

The state of manmukh is one from which only Divine Grace can provide deliverance.

6

The Goal of Liberation

If this were a detective novel there would now be so many clues in the reader's hands that no mystery would be left. Such was Guru Nanak's concern for the unenlightened that diagnosis, warning of a need for radical change, and remedy, are often found together, like nettles and dock leaves in the British countryside. There are, however, a number of terms that must be examined in considering the solution. The first of these is mukti or moksha, both words are used. They mean spiritual enlightenment or liberation. Translations often use the word 'salvation' but it is not preferred here because it can result in students bringing with them concepts from other, usually so-called western, religious traditions. Liberation is from darkness, self-centredness, falseness (i.e. maya, haumai, and the condition of manmukh), the consequence of which is death as with all diseases that are not cured, and rebirth into this worldly existence, possibly in other life forms.

Gurmukh

Those whose outlook and lives have been transformed by God's grace are said to be gurmukh, literally, 'one whose face is turned to the Guru.' (This term should not be confused with Gurmukhi, literally 'from the Guru's mouth', the name given to the script in which Punjabi is written.) Such a person is one who is 'rid of haumai and in whose mind, 'man', through the Divine Word [Shabad], the immaculate Name [Nam] abides' (AG 1342). Her or his life is devoted to meditating upon Nam and serving the Guru in the form of humanity. The full significance of the terms mentioned in this paragraph will be brought out in the following pages.

Bhai Gurdas provides this contrast between the manmukh and gurmukh:

> As the smell of garlic and musk is different, gold and iron are not the same. Glass crystal is not equal to diamond and, likewise, sugar cane and a hollow reed are not the same. Red and black seed are not equal to jewels and glass cannot sell for the

price of an emerald. Evil intellect is a whirlpool but the wisdom of God [gurmat], is the ship of good deeds that takes one across [the world-ocean]. An evil person is always condemned and the good person is applauded by all. Through the gurmukh truth becomes manifest and so is known by one and all, but in the manmukh the same truth is suppressed and concealed. Like a broken pot, it is of no use. (Var 31, Pauri 11)

Of the gurmukh he writes:

> Rivers and small streams joining the Ganges become that sacred river. With the touch of the philosopher's stone all mixed base metals are transformed into gold. Vegetation, fruitful or fruitless, has the scent of sandalwood by assimilating in to itself the fragrance of sandal. In the six seasons and twelve months nothing except the sun is there. Four varnas and six schools of philosophy, and twelve sects of yogis are in this world but by treading the path of gurmukhs all the dualities in the above sects vanish. Gurmukhs with stable minds adore the One. (Var 5, Pauri 9)

The contrast between the manmukh and gurmukh, self-centred and God-centred, is clearly brought out in these words:

> Man comes into this world destined to death. The invaluable human existence is lost in duality. He does not understand himself and weeps through doubt. The saint tells, reads, and hears of the One. The support of the earth blesses him with fortitude, righteousness and protection. If the mortal is at ease in this fourth state, then chastity, righteousness and self-control are enshrined in his 'man'. (AG 686)

Again Bhai Gurdas might be quoted:

> The Gurmukh moves upon the simple and straight way and the manmukh goes astray on twelve ways [the twelve sects of yogis]. Gurmukhs get across whereas the manmukhs get drowned in the world-ocean. The gurmukh is the sacred pool of liberation and manmukhs go on transmigrating and suffering the pangs of life and death. The gurmukh is at ease in the Divine Court but the manmukh has to bear the rod of Yama, the god of death. The gurmukh forsakes ego, whereas the manmukh burns himself continuously in the fire of egoism. Rare are the people who, though being in the limits of maya, remain immersed in meditation on God. (Var 5, Pauri 15)

He also taught that the gurmukh improves this life and is given an exalted place in God's court. He laughs as he goes and does not weep at the end (Var 17, Pauri 14, and Var 19).

Mukti

Mukti or moksha is the condition of those who are cured or made whole. This is perhaps the most apt statement that can be made as mukti consists of the negative, being delivered from as well as being released to a new, spiritually healthy, wholesome and blissful existence. It is very difficult to find passages that describe mukti. One of the more explicit reads:

> Among all beings there is light. You are that light. By God's light, the light shines in everyone. By the Guru's teaching the light becomes manifest. Whatever pleases God is real worship. (AG 663)

Generally these passages link the term with the condition or state from which release is obtained, and with the prescribed remedy and resulting conduct. For example:

> The thoughtful person takes a step after thoughtful consideration. Forsaking duality he becomes a worshipper of the formless One. He obtains the wealth of liberation and enjoys God's elixir. Coming and going end and he is protected by the Guru. Abandoning the ocean, the swan goes nowhere else. Embracing devotion [bhakti], he merges in the One. (AG 663)

Faith leading to practice is an essential prerequisite of liberation.

> There is no liberation without dwelling on God's Name. (AG 663)

> Lay aside greed, and love God so that you may find the door to liberation. (AG 1030)

> Liberation comes through truthful living. (AG 141)

This is not a suggestion that a life of virtue is all that is needed. The Guru also said:

> The virtuous disfigure their meritorious acts by asking for the door of liberation. Those who call themselves continent leave home and hearth but do not know the way of life. Everyone

considers himself perfect. None describes himself as lacking [virtue]…You are known by the grace of the Guru through whom you reveal yourself. (AG 469)

For the Sikh mukti is an active noun. The liberated person behaves in certain ways. Nam simran (see below) is one, but this has to be combined with sewa, the service of humanity. It is said that Nehru, India's first prime minister, declared 'Aram haram hai', 'to rest is forbidden', and that he had in mind religious people who left home, village and work behind to live as recluses in the forest. Nam simran and sewa must be characterised by a positive attitude to worship and labour. In a well-known aphorism Guru Nanak says:

> Virtuous conduct may result in a better incarnation; mukti comes only from the grace of the Sat Guru. (AG 2)

Jivan Mukt

This is one of the most distinctive and important concepts of Sikhism, though, of course, in various ways, it can be found in other forms of spirituality. Nevertheless, the belief that one can be liberated here and now is a powerful one.

Guru Nanak accepted the Hindu concept of a cyclical rather than linear form of history. Though creation emanated from Akal Purukh because of the Divine Hukam, there is no eschatology. History may be terminated, again by God's Hukam, but the Sikh Gurus did not discuss this. They were far more interested in the spiritual liberation of humanity than in speculation upon the cosmic future of the universe, or even the earth. The world, as we have seen, is condemned to coming and going, transmigration, until humanity becomes liberated. In this context it is not surprising to find Guru Nanak stressing the concept or status of *jivan mukt*, being freed from rebirth, enlightened and emancipated in this life. The jivan mukt should accumulate no further karma and at the end of their present life, with all karma from previous births exhausted, they will continue a life of eternal bliss in God. Sikhs often speak of the Gurus going to their 'heavenly abode', rather than dying, for this reason. It is the timeless condition of the 'man', or *jiva* or jot (inner light) which matters, not the necessary temporal state which the body must endure.

> The faces of those who have pondered on Nam and departed on completing their labours, shall be bright and many will be liberated along with them. (AG 8)

Stilling haumai, one practises Simran, penance and self-denial. Hearing the Shabad, one becomes jivan mukt. (AG 1042)

It may be that the comments of the fifth Sikh teacher, Guru Arjan, are among the most helpful and appropriate. Using the imagery of marriage popular among the Gurus, he wrote:

My friends met me and asked me to describe my husband. I was so filled with the bliss of his love that I could not answer them. (AG 459)

The state cannot be expressed only experienced. Those who are jivan mukt realise this and make no attempt at description. To quote Guru Arjan again:

The one who has love of God's command [hukam] in the heart is said to be jivan mukt. Release is a present reality; joy and sorrow are both the same, happiness is eternal. There is no separation from God. Whoever regards success in this world as any enterprise ordained by God, is said to be liberated whilst in the body. (AG 275)

Guru Tegh Bahadur might be regarded as a man who experienced the contrasts of sorrow and joy, dukh and sukh, more than most. Yet he could write:

One who when in grief does not accept grief, is not engrossed in comfort, attachment and fear, realises gold only as dust, untouched by blame or praise, by greed, desire or ego, stays above sorrow and joy, unaffected by acclaim or accusation. Who discards all desire and longing, stays aloof from the world, remains untouched by love and anger, in whose heart the Creator abides. Only that person understands this way of life on whom the Guru [God] showers grace. Nanak says, that person's soul merges with the Divine as water merges with water.

The life of equipoise, *sahaj*, one beyond grief or joy, is the lifestyle of the jivan mukt.

Anand describes a similar state but Sikhs sometimes claim that it is the one word that has no opposite! In the Anand Sahib, Guru Amar Das wrote:

Suffering, sickness and affliction are removed with listening to the True Word. Friends and saints are all fulfilled learning from the True Guru. Those who hear are made pure, those who speak are made pure for they are imbued with the True Guru. Says prayerful Nanak, 'Those who place themselves at the Guru's feet hear the sounds of celestial music.' (AG 922)

7

How Liberation is Obtained

The Remedy

This takes various forms and may be expressed in a number of ways but there is unanimity in the view that it is only through the divine initiative that mukti can be achieved. Instead of being manmukh, self-centred, literally 'one whose face is turned away from God', one must become gurmukh, God-centred, 'one whose face is turned towards God'. How does one who has been transformed by God's grace and hukam respond?

One of Guru Nanak's most famous utterances, which has come to encapsulate a guiding Sikh principle, reads: 'Highest of all [qualities or virtues] is Truth but higher still is Truthful living' (AG 62).

For many, if not most, Sikhs today, Truthful living is learned at home from the family, frequently from the grandmother through stories, such as those already mentioned, and her daily example of Nam simran and going to the gurdwara to pay respect to the Guru Granth Sahib. In the Diaspora where the extended family system may not exist, Truthful living is acquired as it first was in the Guru's own lifetime as a member of a sangat, the local community of believers. It is impossible to overstate the potential of the sangat in helping liberation to be attained. For this reason, among others, there can be no such thing as a Sikh who is individualistic and shuns this fellowship.

Nadar

Sikhism is a religion of grace. Sikh teaching is that 'The body takes birth because of karma but liberation is attained by God's grace' (AG 2). The sound ordering of society demanded a sense of responsibility for one's actions. Thus the Gurus could endorse the belief that 'One reaps what one sows' (AG 662). If, however, this became an article of religious faith, the Gurus realised that there would be little or no place for the liberating activities of God. As in some forms of Hinduism God would merely be an object of devotion. This ran contrary to Sikh experience. Guru Nanak could say that he was 'Neither chaste nor true, not even a scholar, just one born into the world foolish and ignorant' (AG 12). The other Gurus and the masses who became their followers would admit the same. They were not Brahmins or princes but, often, the poorest of the poor. It is only in a religion of grace that they can find hope.

The Gurus used a rich vocabulary in referring to the concept of grace. *Nadar*, a word of Arabic origin, is used of the favourable glance that a superior bestows upon an inferior. Darshan, from the Sanskrit, is the grace in the enlightening glance of a guru that penetrates to the centre of the devotee's being.

Grace is the beginning of a process, involving meditation on God's Name and the shabad; the influence of the sangat and, especially, sewa are means of spiritual development.

> Within us are ignorance, suffering and doubt, but they are cast out by the Guru's wisdom. The one to whom you show your grace and bring to yourself meditates on the Name. You are ineffable, immanent in all. The one you bring to truth attains it. (AG 1291)

There are many significant concepts in the teachings of the Gurus to which attention will now turn but it must always be remembered that Sikhism is not merely a matter of philosophical analysis but a message of spiritual liberation.

Shabad

The concept of 'word' has a long history in Indian religious thought, and it is also important in other religions such as Islam, Judaism, and Christianity. 'The Word of God' is an important phrase in all of them but no more so than in the teachings of Guru Nanak and his successors.

Occasionally, the word is linked with anahad or similar Punjabi expressions. *Anahad shabad* occurs six times in Guru Nanak's writings, for example:

> The anahad shabad is obtained through the wisdom of discernment imparted by the Guru. Through the gurbani, anahad is procured and thus haumai is annulled. (AG 21, see also 351)

Anahad means 'unstruck' in Sanskrit. It is divine in origin, composed by no human agent, and thus signifies something pure or immaculate. It is used in Tantra and Hatha yoga but not necessarily in connection with Divine Reality. In Sikhism the context is invariably theistic. To say that 'God is absorbed in the anahad shabad' is to express an intimacy between Akal Purukh and the shabad. Thus Guru Nanak can say that 'the shabad alone is eternal and that all else is perishable' (AG 155). He is being critical of the dress and ways of the yogi, which can avail nothing in terms of mukti.

The most important thing about the shabad is what it does rather than an analysis of what it is. It is a means of revelation. Through the shabad, the impenetrable Divine represented by the anahad, which could only be realised in experience, becomes the Word which can be communicated to human beings. The inexpressible takes form; nirguna becomes saguna.

> What can I say with one tongue? No one has found your limit. Those who meditate on the true shabad merge into you...The Guru's Word [shabad] is the jewel which discloses the True One by shedding Divine Light. (AG 1290)

> The Supreme Creator has created the fickle world of vegetation and by the shabad has revealed the wondrous show. (AG 1037, cf. 1038)

> You are Akal Purukh, death has no power over your head. You are ineffable, inaccessible and detached. You, the shabad, are true, content, and very cool. One is attuned to you through a calm and cool temperament ...The Immaculate Light is the life of the whole world. By the Guru the anahad shabad is realised. (ibid.)

The state of equipoise is not necessarily ecstatic or trance-like. Guru Nanak links the shabad with sewa. The truly liberated person inevitably serves humanity:

> Meeting the Sat Guru one is blessed with right understanding and remains merged in the love of Nam. Through the shabad truth one practises truth and sings the true songs [bani] and God's praise'...Without serving the Guru [Gursewa] one cannot meditate on God, even if one makes many efforts. (AG 1342)

Gursewa is understood by Sikhs to refer to the service which they should perform in the community and society in general, the manifest form of the Guru, God. In the words of Bhai Gurdas:

> God is beyond taste and words; how can the ineffable story be told by the tongue? God is beyond praise, and slander does not come in the periphery of telling and hearing. God is beyond smell and touch and the nose, and the breath is also wonder-struck but cannot be known. He is away from any varna and symbolism and is even beyond the sight of concentration. Without any support God resides in the grandeur of

earth and sky. The holy congregation is the abode of truth where, through the word of the Guru, the formless One is recognised. The whole of creation is a sacrifice to the Creator. (Var 16, Pauri 12)

Hukam

Together with shabad and nam, and guru, is the word hukam. It means order or command. Someone might say, 'Hukam karo', 'give me your instructions, tell me what you want me to do.' Also, it is customary in gurdwaras or a Sikh home to take the hukam, God's order for the day, a random verse prayerfully chosen. Sometimes it will be written in chalk on a blackboard or typed and displayed on the noticeboard so that devotees coming to pay their respects to God in the Guru Granth Sahib may know what it is. The hukam from the Golden Temple in Amritsar is available daily on the Internet. Hukam is the antithesis of maya and haumai, which are centred upon self-gratification. Hukam implies doing the will of others, God or the sat sangat. (It does not matter that the hukam from one place, say home, may differ from that in a local gurdwara. God's overall will is one, but it can vary between individuals and groups.) The term is often associated with nam, shabad and guru. For example:

> They whom God causes to abide by his hukam, place the shabad in their hearts. Such are God's true brides who love their spouse. (AG 72)

All that happens is the result of God's will, hukam. On the very first page of the Japji we read:

> How can we be true and how can the screen of untruth be rent? By obeying the Ruler's hukam. By the hukam bodies are produced. The hukam cannot be described. Through hukam souls come into existence and by hukam greatness is obtained. By the hukam mortals are made high and low and by his written hukam they obtain good or ill. Some obtain gifts by God's hukam, others are made to wander in transmigration for ever. All are subject to hukam, no one is exempt. O Nanak, if one were to understand the hukam no one would live according to haumai. (AG 1)

> God gives food and drink, whatever befalls a person through God's will and command should be endured with equanimity. (AG 434)

Nam

Literally translated as 'Name', students of religion and devotees will realise the inadequacy of such a rendering. In the Christian and Jewish traditions, especially, but also Hindu, Name has power; and beyond the great religions many ancient myths narrate the hold which one has once an adversary's name is known. Personal names are chosen with great care in many cultures and their meanings are known. Sikhs should consult the Guru Granth Sahib when naming a child, and are encouraged to use the surname Kaur for women and Singh for men instead of the family name, which immediately indicates the zat to which a person belongs and can lead to social discrimination. Nam is to be found 715 times in the bani of Guru Nanak alone. It occurs on almost every page. Guru Nanak uses the word Nam almost as a synonym for shabad: 'Through the shabad one keeps Nam in mind ... Through God's Name one is blessed with the sublime state of bliss' (AG 1342). Here 'God's Name' is a translation of the phrase 'Ram Nam'. The Guru uses a Hindu name for God. (One's attention is drawn to the chant 'Ram Nam satya hai' when a body is being taken to the cremation ground, or to Gandhi's dying words 'Hai Ram'.)

Nam is also the agent of creation: 'The self-existent God became manifested in Nam. Second came the creation of the universe. God pervades it and revels in the creation' (AG 463).

Nam is mainly known, however, as the necessary spiritual liberator and enlightener. First, Nanak uses an agricultural metaphor, then he speaks of the parlous state of a blind man trying to find his way in a dark, moonless night. Transmigration is the inevitable consequence of forgetting Nam.

> God first prepares the mind and then sows the seed of the True Nam. From the Nam of the One the nine treasures are produced and the mortal comes to bear the mark of grace ... The blind man has forgotten Nam. A perverse person walks in pitch darkness. His coming and going does not cease and he is ruined in death and rebirth. (AG 19)

Nam is latently immanent in human beings, but the seeker must abandon maya and haumai. This is compatible with the belief that some effort is needed by one who seeks liberation. When the Guru says that it is possible to forsake Nam or that life is futile without it, he is saying that Nam must be realised to be effective.

> Utter truth and realise God who is within. God is not far off and may be seen by casting a glance... Within the body abides

Nam. My soul does not die. Through the shabad the Divine will is realised. (AG 1026)

Without Nam no one is anything. The perfect Guru has perfected my mind. I am brimful of demerit and have no virtue. Without virtue how can I reach my home? Through Nam equipoise and peace well up. Without destiny the wealth of Nam is not gained. Those within whose minds Nam does not abide have no place of rest. They are bound down and endure hardship. Why have those who have forgotten Nam been born? They obtain no peace here or in the hereafter. Their carts are laden with ashes. (AG 1010)

It is apparently possible to turn away from Nam, to return to the state of manmukh; hence, the need to associate constantly with the sangat.

Without Nam life is futile. With it the devotee has a new vision of Reality. At the end of the passage in which he described his experience of being 'taken to God's Court' (AG 150), he affirms that: 'Since then, the True Nam has become my ambrosial food [amrit]', and continues, 'Those who eat this food to their satisfaction obtain happiness [peace, bliss].' Birth is futile without Nam (AG 1127), so an earnest prayer is that he may be blessed with Nam (AG 1291).

The full significance of Nam is communicated on the same page of the Adi Granth and demonstrates why the Guru sought its blessing, but the contiguity is probably coincidental or the result of an editorial decision by Guru Arjan. It reads:

By your Nam man is ferried across [the world-ocean, i.e. delivered from rebirth], by your Nam he is honoured and adorned. Your Nam is the jewellery of the awakened mind. Through your Nam all names are celebrated. Without Nam man never gathers honour. All other cleverness is a false show. Whoever is blessed with Nam accomplishes his tasks. Your Nam is my power and support. Your Nam is my army and sovereign. Through your Nam one is approved with honour and glory. By your grace one is stamped with your blessing. By your Nam the mortal is blessed with equipoise and by your Nam with your praise. Your Nam is the nectar which purges man of the poison of mammon...The whole world is involved in sin, O my Creator, your Nam alone is the cure for all ills.

It may not come as too much of a surprise to find Guru Nanak addressing those who fail to seek Nam in a threatening manner:

What can the poor, awestricken, god of death [Yama], do to the Gurmukh [those oriented towards the Guru], within whose mind the Enemy of ego abides? May the life bereft of Nam be burnt. By the Guru's grace I contemplate and remember and tell his rosary [japmala], and my 'man' enjoys his flavour. (AG 1332)

It is essential, however, for Nam to become a reality in a person's life.

Nam simran, Nam japna

These phrases are used to describe the technique by which the Sikh consciously realises God. Like the words 'prayer' or 'worship', there is a danger of the activity being thought of as a simple, repetitive exercise. This is far from true. Nam simran may mean remembering God or calling God to mind, and Nam japna is, literally, repeating Nam, but the practices are quite complex. Nam japna may consist of meditating upon a word like 'Waheguru' (or 'Vahiguru'), meaning 'Praise to the Guru', but now used as a popular name for God. Bhai Gurdas explained the Vahiguru Mantra thus:

In the Satyug in the form of Vasudev is said to have incarnated the 'V' of Vahiguru the reminder of Vishnu. The True Guru of dvapar is said to be Harikrishna and 'h' reminds them of Hari. In the Treta age was Ram, and the 'R' of Vahiguru says that remembering Ram will produce joy and happiness. In the Kalyug, Gobind is in the form of Nanak and 'g' of Vahiguru gets Govind recited. The recitations of all the four ages subsume in the soul of the common man. When joining the four letters of Vahiguru is remembered, the jiv [soul] merges again in its origin. (Var 1, Pauri 49)

Some scholars do not subscribe to the views propounded here and consider the passage to be an interpolation. Vah Guru, 'Praise to the Lord', occurs frequently in the Janam Sakhis, including the easily accessible B40, sometimes as an exhortation at the end of a section: 'Bolahu Vahi Guru', 'Cry praise to the Guru'. On page 175, Guru Nanak instructed Mardana to recite 'Vahi Guru' as he kneaded cakes of rice and flour. Water and fire for preparing and cooking the cakes had been refused by the people who provided the flour. They appeared miraculously when Mardana repeated the expression. Clearly, here it is used as a charm. Today it is invoked as a popular name for God, that is Nam, and may be chanted as a form of Nam simran. This usage has its origins in the Janam Sakhis.

Sikhs who really practise Nam japna strive consciously to become one with the Divinity who is within their being. So it is with Nam simran, but here the emphasis is often upon the bani. Each morning the devotee should dwell upon the Japji, for example, which, significantly, is not set to a musical raga or measure. It may sometimes be recited by a group of people, but more often than not it is reflected upon early in the day after bathing, at amrit vela (between 3 a.m. and 6 a.m.), the period of the night when all is still, body and mind are rested, the cares of the day may be some way ahead, and conditions are conducive to meditation. In the Japji itself, these words occur, preceded by a rhetorical question:

> Seekers forever seek gifts and the giver gives more and more. What can we offer for a glimpse of the Court? What can we say to win divine love? In the ambrosial hour [amrit vela] exalt and reflect upon the True Name [Sach Nam]. (AG 2, see also AG 227)

Nam simran dispels the wretchedness which comes from living a life based on self, haumai. Nam simran helps one to suppress self: 'Stilling haumai, one practises simran, penance and self-denial. Hearing the Shabad, one becomes jivan mukt, deathless in life' (AG 1042).

Rather differently expressed but having the same fundamental meaning are these words:

> When one is rid of duality one realises the shabad and within and without knows that God is one. This alone is sublime counsel and instruction. Being engrossed in duality ashes fall on one's head. To become gurmukh and praise God is the sublime deed. With the saints dwell on God's virtues and Divine Knowledge. Whosoever overcomes the 'man' realises death in life. Nanak, through grace the gracious One is recognised. (AG 1343)

The Guru's life was one of continuous longing for Nam, a realisation which was not a once and for all time experience:

> As you keep me so I live; whatever you give me to eat, I eat. As you drive me so I am driven; I enshrine your ambrosial Nam within my mouth. All glories are in your hands. My heart's yearning is that you unite me with yourself. (AG 1012)

The practice of simran would originally have been taught by the Guru to his chelas or Sikhs. Now it should be acquired through the example of parents and the sangat, or *sants* who are (almost always) spiritually enlightened men who attract devotees seeking a living guide. They are not gurus and their teaching should be the gurbani, though there may be a particular emphasis, such as the importance of following the discipline of the Khalsa or a vegetarian lifestyle. It requires discipline, not merely rising early but control of the mind so that concentration can be solely on the Word, on Nam. Perhaps as good a summary as any is given by Guru Nanak on page 597 of the Guru Granth Sahib:

> O creator, you are the honour of me, the one without honour. In my lap is the honour and glory of the wealth of Nam. I am merged in the True Shabad ...Day, night and morning my 'man' remains imbued in you and my tongue repeats your praise. You are True and I am absorbed in you, having realised the mystery of the shabad I have ultimately become true. They who day and night are imbued with Nam are pure. They who come and go are impure. I know no other like my God who has no equal. Who else should I praise? I am a slave to God's slaves, and know God through the Guru's instruction. (AG 597)

In addition to morning and evening practice of Nam simran, many Sikhs constantly call God to mind as Guru Nanak did. 'Day, night, and morning' are not merely to be taken literally. 'Slaves' is used to mean the sangat and 'praise' to mean the singing of the shabad. These are important forms of Nam simran which aid the Sikh in becoming gurmukh.

Nam itself has been discussed in the previous section, now it must be considered in its practical, spiritual context. For Nanak, it was an experiential imperative: 'By repeating Nam I live, forgetting it I die.' A few lines further on we read: 'O Nanak, without Nam, mortals are outcaste wretches' (AG 349).

Sangat

There can be no such person as an individualistic Sikh. Wholeness and unity characterises his vision and teaching. As there is one God so is there one humanity. In the Janam Sakhis it is recorded that wherever the Guru went he established a dharamsala. This was not a building as much as a place where a congregation met, just as today a gurdwara should not be regarded as a building, much more a place where the Guru Granth Sahib is installed and men and women gather around it to worship and provide mutual support and perform sewa. Of the sangat, Nanak, who held it in very high esteem, when asked

'How can the society of saints be recognised?' replied: 'The Nam of the One is uttered there' (AG 72). 'Saints' is a popular translation for 'sangat' or 'sat sangat', but the word saint should not be regarded as it is in other religious traditions and especially some forms of Christianity. The usage is synonymous with a community of believers.

There is no suggestion in the Guru's words that gurmukh, or God-oriented people, only appeared when his ministry began. They have existed for as long as men and women responded to Nam.

> The Sat Guru is near, not far away. The gurmukhs understand this through grace. There is profit in associating with them day and night. This is the glory of the Guru's sangat. Your saints are sublime in every age. Happily they sing God's praise with their tongues. Uttering God's praise they are rid of pain and poverty and fear no one. They remain awake and are not found to be asleep. By serving truth they save the sangat and their lineage. (AG 1025)

> The Guru's servants are loved by the Sat Guru. They meditate on the shabad and sit on the throne. They obtain the quintessence and know the state of their inner selves. Such is the true glory of those who join the sat sangat. God's slave saves himself and his ancestors too. (AG 1026)

The sangat must be completely focused on God: 'Only they are saints who fix their minds on the True One' (AG 1342). The sangat exists to worship and to serve. Sewa, as is noted several times elsewhere, is an obligation which Sikhs recognise and take seriously.

> All the world continues coming and going. Those who seek a seat in God's court should dedicate themselves to the service of people in this world. (AG 26)

The saints must be God-oriented, they are not a group who call themselves followers of the Guru: 'They alone are the sangat who fix their minds on God' (AG 1342). But the person who is a member of the sangat will be greatly blessed.

> Rare are persons whom God assays and consigns to the treasury. They rise above jati and varna and do away with earthly love and avarice. They who are imbued with Nam are the pure pilgrimage places. They are rid of the filth and ailment of haumai. Nanak washes the feet of those Gurmukhs who love the True One. (AG 1354)

The sangat is a major source of liberation:

Those who have pondered on Nam and departed on completing their labours, their faces shall be bright and many shall be liberated along with them. (AG 8)

Yet again a terse aphorism is offered, stressing the importance of the faith community:

If you wish to cross the water, consult those who understand the art of swimming. (AG 1410)

Kirtan

The visitor to a gurdwara when worship is taking place will immediately hear the singing of hymns from the scriptures. The congregational singing of God's praise is an exercise which Guru Nanak considered very important. It is known as kirtan or shabad kirtan. It originates from his emphasis on the sat sangat, the assembly of those who are given to professing Truth and the One Nam. The basis of this are his hymns (bani), though in the Guru Granth Sahib there are also some compositions by Kabir, Sheikh Farid, Namdev, Ravidas, and other north Indian saints. It is possible, though a matter of argument, that these were collected by Guru Nanak and used devotionally by the Kartarpur community. Hymn singing is the easiest way to communicate and imbibe religious teaching. The truth of this was not lost upon the Guru who travelled with Mardana singing God's praises wherever they went. He taught:

Singing and listening to temporal music, the 'man' is attached to duality. Within is deceit and he suffers great pain. Meeting the Guru he is blessed with right understanding and sings the true bani and God's praise...Without serving the Guru [Gursewa], no one can meditate on God, no matter how much they try. (AG 1342)

In gurdwaras worldwide kirtan forms a major part of worship though usually it is left to semi-professional musicians known as ragis to do the singing and provide any exposition of the hymns. This marks an important shift from the practice of participation by the whole congregation which was encouraged by Guru Nanak.

A description of life in the Kartarpur community is pertinent here. The life of other communities would be modelled on it.

When Baba Nanak uttered hymns light would spread and darkness be dispelled. Discussions for the sake of knowledge and the melodies of unstruck music were heard there continuously. Sodar and Arti were sung and in the ambrosial hours Japji was recited. The Gurmukh [Nanak] saved the people from the clutches of Tantra and the Atharva Veda. (Var 1, Pauri 38)

Tantric Hinduism cannot easily be defined but here it is only necessary to explain why Guru Nanak was opposed to its teachings and techniques, matters that were taken up in his discussion with the Siddhs, in his lengthy composition, Siddh Gosht. Exponents of Tantra taught, as he did, that one might become jivan mukt, but through the exercise of yogic practices which were intended to awaken the kundalini. This was latent power akin to a sleeping serpent, situated behind the genitals, and yogic techniques enabled it to pass through a number of chakras (discs) in the spine until it reached the susumna at the top of the cranium, the fontanelle. This done, the Tenth Door, often mentioned by Guru Nanak, opened, and the spirit attained sahaj, blissful union with Brahman. Techniques involved asceticism but also, on the other hand, extreme sexual acts. It was the latter combined with the idea that union could be forced by human will and action that made Tantra unacceptable. It seemed to negate all that the Gurus taught. Though the Gurus might mention the Tenth Door, they did not share the tantric interpretation.

Having described, in this section, how a person might become gurmukh or jivan mukt, it may come as a surprise to find that even the desire for mukti might be considered selfish. Guru Arjan, the fifth Guru, wrote:

I desire neither worldly power nor mukti. My soul longs to embrace your lotus feet. There are Brahma, Shiva, yogis and sages, as well as Indra, but I desire nothing but to receive your darshan. (AG 534)

Perhaps less dramatically but with the same emphasis, demonstrating that the origins of the idea lie in the teachings of the Founder, are these words:

I have neither fear of death nor craving for life. I seek only you, O God, who cherishes all and in whose will we breathe and survive. (AG 20)

The person who longs for God's abode is unconcerned about attaining mukti or paradise. (AG 360)

8

The Scriptures

This section will be concerned primarily with the scripture that contains the compositions of the six Gurus through whom God's message was revealed. It is variously described as the Adi Granth and the Guru Granth Sahib. The collection related to the tenth Guru, the *Dasam Granth*, will be examined at the end of the chapter.

'I speak only as I am given to speak [by God]', Guru Nanak once said (AG 722). This sentence may be said to encapsulate the complete theology of the Guru Granth Sahib. From the first day of his ministry when Guru Nanak experienced being taken to the Divine Court, he was conscious of being God's minstrel, not composing his own songs, or expressing his own views, but being the oracle of the One Supreme Reality. He distinguished between himself as a preacher and the message. This may be why he and his successors provide so little biographical information in the Guru Granth Sahib. It contains exclusively the shabad, or gurshabad, or gurbani (Divine Word). To over-identify messenger and message might be to devalue the unique significance of the revelation that they received.

The Guru Granth Sahib is, however, a corpus of spiritual compositions given its final form by the tenth Guru, who included none of his own works (though some Sikhs consider one couplet to be his), and containing the writings of the first five Gurus, the ninth, those of some Sikh bards, and the *bhagat* bani, material by such non-Sikhs as Kabir, Baba Farid, and Ravidas.

When this written text first came to exist is uncertain. By the time of his death Guru Nanak had composed 947 hymns, some admittedly of only two lines but the majority of considerable length. Many of these could be preserved in the minds of devotees, such is the emphasis upon accurately committing texts to memory in eastern societies, but there were considerations pointing to the need to provide copies of his writings. One would be the deaths of leading members of the community, another would be to meet the spiritual requirements of Sikhs living at a distance from Kartarpur and later the village where Guru Angad established his gaddi. In the times of the fourth and fifth Gurus there was also a real danger of rival claimants to the guruship perverting scripture to enhance their own claims to leadership or their heretical teachings. Perhaps Guru Nanak's sons posed such a threat.

Tradition favours Guru Angad as the inventor of the gurmukhi script in which the Guru Granth Sahib is written, drawing on alphabets familiar to businessmen, but scholars are not in agreement as to whom should be given the credit. It certainly seems likely that Guru Nanak would have been involved in the preservation of what he regarded as sacred scripture.

With the exception of the Japji of Guru Nanak, the rest of the Guru Granth Sahib was set to well-known Punjabi tunes or ragas, finally by Guru Arjan, though of course Guru Nanak and Mardana would have used such tunes as they took their message from village to village.

The Goindval or Mohan *Pothis* are the earliest known collections of the scriptures. It is said that Guru Amar Das had the writings of himself and his predecessors, as well as those of the bhagats, copied out by his grandson, Sahans Ram. They existed in three or four volumes or pothis as they were commonly called. They subsequently came into the possession of Mohan, son of Guru Amar Das, hence their alternative title. A pothi which claims to be the original one exists in the private ownership of a family who are kin of Guru Amar Das. The Goindval Pothis belong to another family of the same sub-caste. The Mohan Pothis were among the texts used by Guru Arjan when compiling the Adi Granth.

From 1603 to 1604 Guru Arjan prepared the book which eventually received the title Adi Granth. His sources were the memories of the long-lived disciple of Guru Nanak, Bhai Buddha, already well into his nineties, and such writings as he could lay his hands on. Besides the hymns of Guru Nanak and Angad (62), Amar Das (907) and his father, Ram Das (679), he added his own considerable corpus of 2,218 as well as the hymns of the Sikh bards and bhagats. Sikhs brought other compositions to him asking that they might be included. The amanuensis was his kinsman, Bhai Gurdas, and the work took place beside the tank of nectar at Amritsar. When it was completed, the volume was installed in the Harimandir Sahib, Guru Arjan prostrating himself before it to demonstrate its status as the eternal Word of God. It came to be known as the Adi Granth, that is the Primal Collection.

The Adi Granth becomes the Guru Granth Sahib

In 1706 Guru Gobind Singh decided to add the bani of his father, the martyr Guru Tegh Bahadur, another 116 passages, some shabads but mostly two-lined shloks. Two years later, just before he died, the Guru declared that there would be no further human Gurus, his successor would be the scriptures, known henceforward as the Guru Granth Sahib.

Structure of the Guru Granth Sahib

The structure of the Adi Granth was imposed by Guru Arjan and followed by Guru Gobind Singh when he added his father's bani. Using for simplicity's sake the 1,430 page numbers of present-day printed versions, we can say that the first thirteen, containing the hymns that Sikhs use every day in their personal devotions, were not placed within the arrangement given to the rest of the book. Pages 14 to 1352 are divided into thirty-one sections, each named after the musical setting or raga to which they should be sung. The last seventy-eight pages contain passages that are too short, often only two lines in length, to be placed satisfactorily within the body of the text. Within each raga, compositions are arranged in a regular order, first those of Guru Nanak, then those of the second, third, fourth, fifth and ninth Gurus; then compositions by Kabir, Farid, Namdev, Ravidas and the other non-Sikh bhagats. The passages by the bards are scattered in various sections and need not concern us here. Not even Guru Arjan is represented in every section.

On page 1429, the subsequent list of ragas on page 1430 is preceded by the verse Mundavani composed by Guru Arjan, which sums up Sikh belief about the importance of the scripture.

> In this thali [dish] are placed three things: truth, content-ment, and meditation. The nectar-Name of God, the support of everyone, has also been put in it. Whoever eats this food, whoever relishes it, becomes spiritually liberated.

The Bhagat Bani

A distinctive feature of the Guru Granth Sahib is the fact that 938 out of 5,894 shabads were composed by non-Sikhs. They include Brahmins, Ramanand and Jaidev, and low-caste men such as Ravidas, a cobbler, Sena, a barber, and Sadhna, a butcher. There was also the Muslim, Sheikh Farid, and at least one person who would not wish to be included in any sectarian grouping, Kabir. The significance of the bhagat bani is two-fold, hence the attention given to it here. First, it provides evidence of a universalist strain in Sikh teaching. This will be examined at greater length as we look at the attitude of Sikhism towards other religions. Second, it is a clear way of affirming the doctrine that the gurshabad was not the exclusive property of Sikhs.

It was probably Guru Nanak who began to collect the compositions of the non-Sikh sants as they are often called. There is one important piece of evidence to support this assertion, and there may be others. It is a verse from Sheikh Farid that occurs in the Guru Granth Sahib, which is cited elsewhere by Guru Nanak himself. Farid's verse reads:

> You could not make a raft at the time you should have made it. When the sea is full and overflowing it is hard to cross. Do not touch the saffron flower with your hand. Its colour will fade, my dear.

> First, the bride herself is weak and, in addition, her husband's command is hard to bear. As the milk does not return to her breast so the soul does not enter the same body again. Says Farid, O my friends, when the spouse calls, the soul departs crestfallen and this body becomes a heap of ashes. (AG 794)

Guru Nanak's rejoinder is:

> Make meditation and self-control the raft by which you cross the flowing stream. Your path shall be as comfortable as if there were no ocean or overflowing stream. You name alone is the unfading madder with which my cloak is dyed. My beloved, this colour is everlasting. The dear friends have departed how shall they meet you? If they are united in virtue they will, and once united mortals never suffer separation again. The True One puts an end to coming and going. (AG 729)

It is impossible to doubt that Guru Nanak was aware of Farid's verse. The fact that they are not adjacent to one another in the Guru Granth Sahib is to be explained by the fact that Guru Arjan had his own reasons for placing passages where he did when he compiled the collection. His reason for separating the verses is unknown.

Whether or not Guru Nanak collected the whole of the bhagat bani cannot yet be decided. Much of the bhagat bani is in one of the Mohan Pothis but not all of it, so it was clearly not Guru Arjan's decision to collect it. Sometimes the suggestion is made that Guru Amar Das may have collected some of it. All that can be said with certainty is that the idea came from Guru Nanak. The reason for including the bhagat bani in a Sikh anthology may well have been to give practical affirmation to the basic Sikh belief that God's word is not confined to any particular religion or spiritual movement. It could also have had the effect of creating sympathy towards the Sikh movement, eventually perhaps leading to membership, from people who venerated the teachings of Sheikh Farid, Kabir and the other teachers. The fact that no material from brahminical Hindu scriptures or the Qur'an is included is easily explained. Either it could result in the charge that the Gurus were merely plagiarists or to the assertion that they did accept the authority of these scriptures. What they certainly were is eclectic in their view of scripture, refusing to claim that God spoke only through the revelation which was given to them. Although historical developments have led to the rule that only expositions of the Sikh scriptures may be given in gurdwaras, references to the sacred books of other religions may be made so long as it is with respect.

The Dasam Granth

Guru Gobind Singh probably did not include any of his many spiritual poetic compositions in the Guru Granth Sahib. These were collected by one of his companions, Bhai Mani Singh, in 1734. The title given to this anthology, which includes some writings by poets who served at the Guru's court, is Dasam Granth. It means 'Collection of the tenth Guru'. In modern printed versions it is 1,428 pages long. There was no attempt of course to emulate the length of the Adi Granth, which, before printing, varied considerably in length depending on the copyist's handwriting. Even when printing was introduced versions varied in their number of pages until the 1,428-page edition won official approval.

The Dasam Granth may be read in gurdwaras and some of its hymns are used in the initiation ceremony and on other occasions, but its authority is not equal to that of the Guru Granth Sahib for several reasons. It was the Guru Granth Sahib which Guru Gobind installed as Guru and that provides Sikhs with reason enough. However, it is also written in a number of languages to which many Sikhs have no access. Guru Gobind Singh was a scholar as well as a poet and seems to have been at home in the Persian of the Mughal court, the Sanskrit of brahminical Hinduism, Punjabi and other north Indian languages. The language of the Guru Granth Sahib may be difficult for young Sikhs living outside Punjab; the Dasam Granth presents problems for all but the most scholarly Sikhs worldwide.

The writings of Bhai Gurdas and Bhai Nandlal

Bhai Gurdas (1551–1637) was a nephew of Guru Amar Das. He was a famous missionary in the Agra area and a compiler of the Adi Granth.

After Guru Arjan's martyrdom in 1606 and when Guru Hargobind was a prisoner in Gwalior Fort, he and Bhai Buddha were responsible for holding together the Panth. He was also a theologian, historian and poet. He composed a large number of *vars* or epic poems, hymns of praise to God's achievements through the Sikh Panth. These compositions may also be read in gurdwaras, along with those of Bhai Nandlal (1633–1713), a companion of the last Guru.

The importance of the Guru Granth Sahib as demonstrated by Sikh practices

Few religions show the importance of their scripture in practice more than Sikhism does. Most of the allusions to this have been made elsewhere in this book. It is intended to help the reader by placing them together here but details will not be repeated. Important events in the lives of the community, families and individuals focus on the scripture: birth, naming, marriage, and death; initiation into the Khalsa, celebrations of *gurpurbs* and often melas by *akhand paths* and nagar kirtan are also essentially linked with the Guru Granth Sahib.

Translating the Scriptures

An elderly Sikh once spoke of reading the Guru Granth Sahib first of all in an Urdu transliteration. He lived, pre-Partition, in a predominantly Muslim region of the Punjab and was unaware of gurmukhi or Hindi in his childhood. Perhaps once, the issue was one of making the scriptures available in scripts that Sikhs knew.

It was only slowly that the question of translation presented itself. The first partial effort was made by a German scholar named Ernest Trumpp in 1877. It has recently been reprinted. Clearly the author achieved a good standard of reliability. Unfortunately, however, he alienated Sikh religious leaders by his arrogant manner and his insensitive treatment of the volume of scripture that he used. Tradition says that he blew smoke from his cigar over it, almost the most offensive gesture that one could imagine. Most Sikhs have never been able to assess his contribution objectively.

The second name that must be mentioned is that of Max Macauliffe. He served in the Punjab as a government administrator and felt it important to record what he could of Sikhism before it became extinct. In six volumes entitled *The Sikh Religion*, he recorded the traditional version of the biographies of the Gurus and translated their compositions and those of the non-Sikh bhagats, such as Kabir and Farid. His contribution was impressive and his volumes have stood the test of time being never, or only for a short period, out of print. He wrote before the numbered pagination of the Guru Granth Sahib was even considered, so students have to accept the raga titles and find them in the modern versions of scripture based on 1,430 pages.

Notably, both Trumpp and Macauliffe had the English-speaking world in mind, no Sikh gave any consideration to translating the scriptures. The Panth had no need of one and Sikhs were not thinking beyond their own needs. Some of their scholars translated the Japji or the five passages used daily by members of the Panth. Perhaps an awareness of informing the English-speaking world of scholarship was beginning to emerge.

Translating poetry is beset with problems. Rendering religious poetry into a foreign language is much more challenging. Many argue that it cannot be done, and this has been the view of a considerable number of Sikhs.

Once the possibility of translation is accepted, scholars are faced with other issues. In the case of Sikhism these are compounded by the memory of Ram Rai, who was willing to misinterpret the gurmukhi, and Trumpp, who was seen to be denigrating the Sikh tradition through his abuse of the scripture. The Guru Granth Sahib, being poetry, is considered by some Sikhs to be impossible to render into any other language. Then there is the question of how the translation should be expressed, in metre or in prose. One meets Sikhs who vehemently assert that only the original language of the Gurus is acceptable and are surprised that an official translation was ever permitted. In the 1960s, however, the SGPC, no less, sanctioned Man Mohan Singh to undertake the monumental task. The result was an eight-volume translation accompanied by the original gurmukhi and a modern Punjabi version, published between 1962 and 1967. It is to be found in most gurdwara libraries throughout the Diaspora and in many Sikh homes. It has considerable merit but suffers from one fault: the translation, though not poetical, is in the English of the King James version of the Bible, or of Shakespeare. One suspects that the inspiration for producing an English version of the Sikh scripture was that used and beloved by many Christians, the one to which Sikhs would have been introduced in schools and colleges, the only one then available, even though the work of modern translation was gathering pace in England and America. Today the third-generation Diaspora Sikh, who knows little Punjabi and cannot read gurmukhi, does not find archaic English any easier to follow. Something else is needed.

Three privately produced translations must be mentioned. Gopal Singh, one time ambassador to Bulgaria and an official observer to an assembly of the World Council of Churches, published his four-volume metrical translation in the 1960s. He published it himself through his World Book Centre, Delhi. Twenty years later Punjabi University, Patiala, produced a four-volume edition by Trilochan Singh. Although this had the support of the university, it was the personal product of the eminent scholar and so should be classed as privately produced. Both these translations have been found difficult to use because of their poetic form.

Jarnail Singh deserves special mention. He is a Sikh who migrated to Canada and became employed as a civil servant. He taught himself French and embarked upon a French translation of the scripture. It was a costly enterprise for him, although a supporter provided some financial assistance. This kind of venture, a form of seva, is typical of the Sikh spirit.

The Sacred Literature Trust has published a small library of texts. In 1996 an anthology compiled by Professor Nikky Guninder Kaur Singh was published by HarperCollins sponsored by the Sikh foundation, San Francisco. This was an interesting achievement for several reasons. Once again, it was the work of an individual but she was advised by four Sikhs and one western scholar. It was also written in modern English prose of the kind found in contemporary literature. It also attempted to tackle some of the gender issues raised by attempts at translation. God is beyond gender but is certainly not 'it'. It contains the compositions found in most gutkas or nitnems, collections used in daily devotions. The Jap of Guru Gobind Singh is included, but most of the passages are verses used individually or in rituals, for example, the wedding hymn, Lavan.

It is too early yet to assess the impact of this anthology on the Panth, but it has the potential to make a significant contribution to the lives of non-gurmukhi-reading and non-Punjabi-speaking Sikhs in the Diaspora, the readership that it had mainly in mind.

There is no tradition of Sikh scholars being brought together to work on translations as there was, according to tradition, with the Greek Septuagint version of the Hebrew scriptures or with the King James Bible and a number of versions published in the twentieth century.

The Dasam Granth

English versions of the Dasam Granth have been confined to translations of particular compositions, for example the Jap mentioned in a previous paragraph. In 1999, to mark the three hundredth anniversary of the founding of the Khalsa, Professor Jodh Singh and Dr Dharam Singh of Punjabi University, Patiala, published the first complete translation in English: *Sri Dasam Granth Sahib*, Heritage Publications (2 vols.). It has the advantage of providing the gurmukhi text opposite the translation.

9

Ethical Teachings

Sikhism is a profoundly ethical religion. The incidents described in the chapter on the Gurus clearly show that they had no place for forms of spirituality which emphasised enlightenment and liberation, mukti, without social responsibility. This is why they could be so severe on those who practised austerity in their personal quest but did not give alms or serve others. Their path was one of selfishness and they themselves were filled with haumai, self-centredness. To be a disciple of the Guru one had to be gurmukh, literally 'one whose face is turned towards God'. Bhai Gurdas described such a person as one from whom God, the Guru

> eradicates his lust, anger and resistance and has his greed, infatuation and ego erased. [The five cardinal evils, according to Sikh teaching are kam (lust), lobh (covetousness), moh (attachment), krodh (wrath), and ahankar (pride).] Instead the Guru makes him practise truth, contentment, kindness, dharma, that is Nam, charity (Dan), and ablution (Ishnan). Adopting the teachings of the Guru, the individual is called a Sikh. (Var 11, Pauri 3)

This passage conveys the essence of the inner and outer transformation which should characterise a true believer. Dharma in this passage probably refers to spiritual and religious observances, but Dan and Ishnan could also be included as having the same purpose.

The basis of Sikh teaching lies in the oneness of God and humanity. Theology has an intensely practical purpose, the spiritual release of the soul from rebirth. In a discourse with a group of yogis, it is clear that Guru Nanak was intent on bringing his adversaries to accept his teaching on liberation rather than enter into a philosophical debate which might have obscured his message with sophistry.

Sikhism takes the world seriously. In it one finds God, or more precisely, one is found by God. Guru Nanak did not point his followers towards material success, but towards responding seriously, that is altruistically, to the material world. He taught: 'They alone have found the right way who earn through toil and share their earnings with others' (AG 1245).

The consequences of such living could extend beyond this present life: 'One receives hereafter only what one gives here out of honest earnings' (AG 472). An interesting and touching statement says: 'As the herdsman is to the pasture for a short time so is the mortal in the world' (AG 418). The Indian husbandman works hard, probably caring for animals which belong to someone else. Similarly, human beings should be devoted servants of God, but they are mistaken if they think that they have any permanence here. The funeral pyre or grave is much in mind:

> If the departing man has taken some riches with him, then you too should amass wealth. See, understand and realise. Do your dealings, gain your object, lest you should have regrets afterwards. Forsake evil and practise virtue, so you shall obtain the real thing. (AG 418)

Caste

This is not the place to analyse or explain the caste system. Elements important to a study of Sikhism are discussed in the section on family life. The Gurus rejected caste discrimination on the grounds that it unethically divided humanity, which the one God ordained to be a unity.

There is no place for the varnashramadharma or for ritual pollution. There is only one class, humanity, and this included everyone, woman as well as man. The four stages of life were summed up in one, that of *grihastha* or gristhi, the householder, which included all the rest. The family is at the core of Sikhism. As for the goals of life, there is only one, moksha or mukti, which entailed the service (sewa) of others regardless of caste, religion or gender. All others are subsumed in it.

The denial of the innate worth of caste is shown in the following verse:

> When God showers benediction, some rare ones understand God, through the Guru. In his mind the lamp becomes permanent. It is not extinguished by water or wind. Kshatriyas, Brahmins, or Vaishyas, do not find worth by making thousands of calculations. Anyone who lights such a lamp becomes liberated. (AG 878)

It is the divine gift of enlightenment which alone has worth.

What power has caste? It is righteousness that is tested. High-caste pride is like poison held in the hand, from eating it a man dies. (AG 142)

Recognise God's light within everyone and do not ask their caste as there is no caste in the next world. (AG 349)

Here it might be appropriate to warn readers not to introduce the subject of caste into conversations with people of Indian origin. It can harm a burgeoning friendship and result in evasive responses.

Ritual Pollution

This is an acceptable aspect of many religions, including Hinduism, Judaism, Christianity, and Islam. The Gurus were, however, severely critical of it. Their world-view of one God, responsible for the whole created universe and one humanity left no place for a concept that seemed to contradict it by saying, on the one hand, that God differentiated between different parts of creation and, more particularly, some people were inferior to others from the moment of birth until they died. A Brahmin who became impure, perhaps through contact with blood, could undergo cleansing rites. A Shudra or Dalit could not remove his inherent taint no matter how many times he washed, bathed in sacred rivers, or attempted to live an ascetic lifestyle avoiding actions and foods that might convey impurity. His conduct was futile, impure he was born and impure he would die. Rebirth might be into a less desperate situation. According to the strictest teachings of Hinduism, women were also inherently impure and one of the main transmitters of ritual pollution.

The eating of flesh was considered to be a major source of pollution and indeed there are some Sikhs who are vegetarians for this reason or out of respect for all living beings. This is discussed later in the chapter.

Women

The status of Indian women frequently draws disapproving comment from western observers, but it should be realised what lies behind their lives and that almost five hundred years ago Guru Nanak was deploring their treatment. Girls are still considered paraya dhan, a Punjabi phrase which literally means the property of another. Their parents raise them and educate them in the knowledge that at marriage they will enter their husband's home to live with his parents, brothers and other sisters-in-law. Certainly among many Sikhs toing and froing from home to home is continuous. (I know of one family who crashed their two cars and borrowed those of the in-laws with the same result!) On the other hand, a professor told me that if he went to Amritsar he never stayed with his daughter. It might be indiscreet. Her husband's family might accuse his daughter of misconduct in not observing the traditions. Other Sikhs have ridiculed this attitude, regarding it as old-fashioned in the extreme. It does, however, make a point, as does the pathetic greeting of beggar girls asking for alms: 'May you be blessed with sons!'

We need not proceed further into Indian culture regarding women's position. Instead, we will turn to Guru Nanak. He began with his usual basic theological assertion:

> The wise and beauteous Being (Purukh, i.e. God) is neither man nor woman nor bird. 'You are our mother and father, kinsman and brother'.
>
> 'You are our mother and father, we are your children'.

When Guru Nanak uses male-female imagery of the relationship of human beings with God might he be seen as speaking only metaphorically or may he be actually referring to the potential of women to enjoy God-realisation? How is the following verse to be understood?

> The virtuous wife enjoys her Spouse. Why does the vicious one bewail? If she becomes virtuous then she too shall go to enjoy her Spouse. My Spouse is the abode of ambrosia... If the bride remains attached to you, O Spouse, then she shall enjoy. (AG 556)

God is above the distinctions of gender as of caste but the Gurus round on those who despised women and treated them as channels of ritual pollution. The key passage to which Sikhs always refer is

> It is from woman that we are conceived and born. Woman is our lifelong friend who keeps the race going. Why should we despise the one who gives birth to great men? When a wife dies another one is sought. To her the man becomes bound. Why call her evil who gives birth to kings? Woman is born of woman, without her there is no one. Nanak, only the True One is without a mother. (AG 473)

One matter that exercised the Gurus was the practice of female infanticide. As indicated above, a daughter is an expense to her family so there has often been a tendency for some Punjabis to ask the midwife to strangle the girl with the foetal cord at birth. This is denounced in many of the rahit namas, or instructions, given by the Gurus to their followers throughout the history of the movement. Only in 2001, the Akal Takht in Amritsar, a major seat of Sikh authority, decreed that female foeticide was contrary to Sikh teachings. In recent years the balance of female births as opposed to male has diminished to an alarming degree.

Sati, the immolation of women upon their husband's funeral pyres, was rejected by the Panth long before it was officially outlawed in India in 1827. Guru Amar Das, the third Sikh leader said:

> Satis are not those who burn themselves on their husbands' funeral pyres. Satis are those who die from the sheer shock of separation. (AG 787)

These words appear on the same page:

> They too be reckoned satis who live virtuously and contentedly in the service of God who is ever cherished in their hearts. Rising in the morning they remember God.

> Wives burn themselves in the fire with their husbands. If they heartily love their spouse they suffer great bodily and mental pangs already. If they do not love their husbands why should they burn themselves in the fire? Whether the husband be alive or dead such a wife remains far from him.

By the time of Guru Amar Das, the Panth may no longer have had committed enlightened Sikhs as its only members. Many would have come as part of extended families rather than individual converts. They would retain links with their (mainly) Hindu background. For this reason he established a baoli or place for ritual bathing at Goindval, the village where he resided. He also made Diwali a Sikh festival, presumably to try to wean his followers off the Hindu concepts associated with it. In such a situation it is likely that he had some followers for whom the tradition of sati was followed. What it is important to ask is where did his rejection of sati originate? The answer must be that the teachings of Guru Nanak established the principle which he developed.

The life of a widow in Indian society could be tragic: little wonder that at her daughter's wedding her mother expresses the wish, 'May you never be a widow'. Death might almost seem preferable to being regarded as the bringer of misfortune and a source of ritual pollution. In Sikhism widows may remarry, if not they remain respected family members. All marriages should be by mutual consent; child marriages and the giving of dowries are forbidden.

The Rahit Maryada, the Code of Discipline which all Sikhs initiated into the Khalsa must observe, states: Women may also take a leading role in any Khalsa ceremony and act as a granthi in gurdwara worship. The theologian Bhai Gurdas wrote: 'From a temporal and spiritual point of view woman is a man's other half and assists him in attaining salvation'.

The Gurus followed up their words with deeds. Guru Amar Das, as has already been noted, appointed peerahs, women preachers, for work among Muslim women; there is a strong tradition that Mata Jeeto, wife of Guru Gobind Singh, provided the sugar crystals for the first amrit ceremony. Mata Sahib Kaur, another wife, was given the honour of being 'mother of the Khalsa'. Women may be members of the Khalsa and serve on gurdwara committees, enjoying the same status as men, and become granthis, but the old traditions of male dominance remain – as they do in many other communities.

Vegetarianism

The avoidance of meat and other blood products, and blood itself, whether it be from a carcass or a menstruating woman, is related to the issue of purity and pollution which has already been mentioned. In the Panth vegetarianism may be regarded as having an ethical dimension. Khalsa members are forbidden to eat animals slaughtered in the Muslim manner (Rehit Maryada, p.38: Khalsa members may eat only jatka meat, that is meat from an animal which has been killed with one blow of a knife or similar implement). Many Sikhs are vegetarian, but the reason for this might be family tradition. In gurdwaras, langar is invariably a vegetarian meal so that no one may be offended. This is a significant feature of the religion. Whereas in some traditions non-members are excluded from certain religious meals, in Sikhism, on the contrary, these are open to everyone. Such people as high-caste Hindus may refuse to eat alongside someone of a lower caste or partake of food prepared and served by such Sikhs, but it is they who exclude themselves, not the sangat. This is, however, very rare in the Diaspora.

According to the Janam Sakhis, Guru Nanak ate venison on at least one occasion. The Bala-based Janam Sakhis describe him as eating goat. In the verses on pages 1289-90 of the Guru Granth Sahib, he addresses the issue: 'Fools quarrel over flesh, and know neither God nor meditation'. Here we may perceive his reason for raising the issue. There were those in the Hindu community who avoided meat eating because of their ideas of pollution. Muslims would avoid the pig because of the teachings of the Qu'ran and they too associated it with pollution. Guru Nanak had no time for such disputations and actions, any more than he had regarding burial or cremation. It was so easy to quibble over such matters and fail to realise what he considered to be most important – becoming brahmgiani or gurmukh, that is one whom has direct experience of God.

He does not let his case rest there, however. A little further on, he speaks in a way which might shock some of his listeners:

> They are produced from the blood of their mother and father, yet they do not eat fish or flesh. When a man and a woman meet at night they co-habit with flesh. From flesh we are conceived, from flesh we are born, we are vessels of flesh. All creatures have sprung from flesh and the soul has taken its abode in flesh.

He continues:

> Flesh is allowed in the Puranas, flesh is allowed in the Muslim scriptures, and flesh has been used in the four ages [kalpas, or periods of history since the creation]. Flesh adorns sacred festivals and marriage functions, flesh is associated with them. Men, women, kings and emperors spring from flesh.

An explanation for Guru Nanak's rejection of vegetarianism may lie in his hostility to notions of ritual pollution. What was simpler than accepting a meat meal to demonstrate this?

Since his time, meat eating has been a matter of personal or family preference. No one would eat beef, the cow being a sacred animal to Hindus, the majority community. Occasionally, in times of active sectarian hostility Muslims have slaughtered cows and thrown their carcasses into mandirs, just as dead pigs may be used to desecrate mosques, but the cow is usually respected even by groups who do not share beliefs about its sanctity. Namdhari Sikhs believe in a living Guru who has been president of the World Vegetarian Association. All his followers are vegetarian.

Drugs

God's light (jot) has been placed within human beings. Therefore, the body must be treated with respect. This is taken as far as the rejection of circumcision, and, by many Sikhs, the refusal to cut the hair, including body hair. Not surprisingly then, the Khalsa Code of Conduct, forbids the use of alcohol, tobacco and other drugs, except for medicinal purposes. Some members of the Panth who have not been initiated into the Khalsa, do drink alcohol and some, but not many, in the writer's experience, smoke cigarettes. Guru Nanak made a few references to drug taking. He told his disciples that those who deal in the Nectar of Truth have no need of alcohol. Compared with God's Amrit, worldly wines were tasteless (AG 360). His companion, Mardana, saw a correlation between alcohol and immorality: 'Wine causes mortals to commit vice' (AG 553).

The Sikh Householder

Guru Nanak utterly rejected the *varnashramadharma* ideal. For him there was one varna, humanity, which included women and men; there was one ashrama, the householder stage of life; there was one dharma, obligatory upon everyone, the worship of God and the service of humanity.

A passage reproving renunciants, wandering mendicants, yogis, men of learning, ascetics and celibates, all of whom are destined to wander in transmigration, has these words of commendation for the devout family person:

> Pandits, teachers and astrologers are forever reading the Puranas, They do not know that which is within. Brahman is contained in the heart. Penitents perform austerities in the forest and some even live at pilgrimage places, unenlightened they do not understand themselves. For what purpose have they become ascetics? Some by effort succeed in restraining their semen. They are called celibates after truth, and are attached to the Guru's teaching. They hold fast to Nam, Dan and Ishnan, and remain awake in God's meditation. (AG 418)

In supporting the householder way of life, that of a husband and wife, their children and other members of the extended family, it might be argued that the Guru was making a virtue of necessity; that most of his audience, if not all, had no alternative but to toil to live, and to eke out a poor existence at that. He was, however, doing more than face an unpleasant reality, he was affirming that the householder (gristhi/grihasta) life is ordained by God. It makes for social unity and coherence, it should, as the Guru envisaged it, find a place of equal status for man and woman, husband and wife. Bhai Gurdas, interpreting his intentions, saw the wife as a necessary counterpart to the husband and his helper in achieving spiritual liberation. It may be true also of other Indian-originating religious traditions, but it is certainly part of the Sikh way of life that young people should marry. Speaking with Sikh students about what they intend to do after graduation, almost all of them say that their parents are looking for a suitable match. An unemployed, highly qualified Sikh divorcee was asked whether she might contemplate going back to India where she would easily have obtained a chair in her chosen discipline. She replied, 'Not until I'm too old for my parents to look for another husband for me'. Obviously, there are Sikhs who never marry, but the ideal norm is that partners should be found for women and men.

Against the tendency to renounce the world Guru Nanak taught:

> Remain in towns and near the main high roads, but be alert. Do not covet your neighbour's possessions. Without Nam we cannot attain inner peace or still our inner hunger. The Guru has shown me that the real life of the city, the real life of its shops, is the inner life. We must be traders in truth, moderate in our eating and sleeping. That is true yoga. (AG 939)

As the above passage states, there is such a thing as householder ethics – moderation in all things is how it might be expressed. The overemphasis on material possessions will only lead to the neglect of Nam. Elsewhere, he amplifies what it means to live the gristhi life:

> He only is a householder who checks his passions and begs from God meditation, hard work, and self-restraint. The householder who, with his body, gives all he can to the poor, is as pure as the river Ganges. (AG 952)

Guru Nanak did not define what were acceptable occupations for Sikhs to follow although most would seem to have been workers of the land or Khatri businessmen. There were, however, also craftsmen in metal, cloth makers, and carpenters. One way of making a living, which is considered a legitimate practice among some castes, seems to have been rejected from Guru Nanak's day, namely that of begging. Guru Nanak had nothing but scorn for the yogi beggars: 'O yogi...you feel no shame in begging from door to door' (AG 903).

The work ethic is a strong aspect of the religion and seems to be endorsed by the passages quoted above. The householder life did not, in itself, ensure spiritual liberation. Guru Nanak gave this warning: 'Entanglements are mother, father, and the world. Entanglements are sons, daughters and wife. Entanglements are religious ceremonies performed through pride. Entanglements are sons, wife, and another's love in the mind ...', and so the list continues, including worldly love and the wealth which bankers amass, and the Vedas and religious discussions. Finally, Guru Nanak says: 'He whom the True Guru saves is free from entanglements' (AG 416).

While it seems clear that the way of life which is favoured is that of the householder, it is a means to an end rather than the final goal. It is all too easy for the daily concerns of family members to lead to the neglect of Nam simran, Dan, and Ishnan. This, presumably, is why begging is unacceptable. The Buddhist mendicant may be providing an opportunity for the lay person to perform a good deed, but normally begging is an act of self-centredness.

Sewa and Langar

Sikhism endorses and teaches a way of life committed to the service of one's fellow human beings. This might be said to be characteristic of many inhabitants of the subcontinent, but it is built into the way of life of Sikhs and, in the author's experience, is unhesitatingly and unstintingly given. Besides being an individual response to the Gurus' teachings, it takes on a corporate aspect in the form of sewa and langar.

The teaching that God's light is in everyone was implemented in a practical way by sewa and the institution of langar. Sewa is service directed to the whole of humanity. To care for one's own family or other Sikhs was not enough. As God's provision had no bounds, so sewa should be unlimited. The Gurus asserted:

'All living beings are your creatures, none can obtain any reward without rendering service [sewa]' (AG 354).

Sewa was not a mere act of temporal concern. It had eternal significance: 'If we want a seat in God's court we should dedicate ourselves to the service of people in this world' (AG 26). 'We shall be rewarded according to the deeds we perform' (AG 468) is considered to have the same meaning. The phrase 'Nam, Dan, Ishnan' was a persistent reminder of the responsibility to serve others, to perform 'Dan'.

One who eats what has been earned through honest labour and from the hand gives some in charity, alone knows the true way of life. (AG 1245)

Sewa, however, has never been putting money in a collection box, though that is also done; it should be something practical which involves women, men, and children, in acts of service. In the Guru's day not many Sikhs may have had money to donate to good causes, but he realised that it is in doing that awareness of the unity of humanity is achieved. Attached to many gurdwaras are dispensaries or even hospitals and eye clinics where people give their services free. Specialist surgeons give time to perform operations. Other Sikhs will cook or clean. It is often in langar that children begin the practice of sewa.

The most famous example of sewa is Bhai Khanayah (his name is spelled in various ways), who lived in the time of Guru Gobind Singh. He cared for wounded men on the battlefield by giving them water, Sikh and Mughal alike. He was taken to the Guru and charged with helping the enemy. He denied this and claimed that he saw God in everyone. The Guru, greatly moved, commended him and encouraged him not only to give water to the needy but also dress their wounds. From his work developed a movement of sewapanthis that still exists.

Langar, or Guru ka langar, is a term found in the Guru's writings and there is a reference to Mata Khivi serving langar (AG 967). It has been suggested that its origins may lie in Sufi Islam, but to defend the uniqueness of the founder Sikhs often dispute and reject the suggestion. The concept is fundamental to his teaching and may be seen as the corollary of sewa. Langar means 'free kitchen' or 'almshouse', a place where anyone may come to be fed. It fits in perfectly with the first Guru's teachings on sewa.

The tradition the practice is based on goes back a long way but today langar is still characterised by three things: pangat, eating in lines sitting on the ground, facing one another; a vegetarian meal, so that no one need feel threatened by the diet provided; and the donation of food by members of the sangat. Responsibility for langar, some giving food, others preparing and cooking it while others serve and wash up – or, where it is served on leaf plates, clear away the debris – is the point where langar and sewa converge. This combination may be hinted at in Pauri 19 of Var 27 by Bhai Gurdas:

> The Sikh of the Guru, falling at his feet, forswears ego and the desires of the mind. He fetches water, fans the congregation, grinds flour and does all manual jobs. He cleanses and spreads the sheets while putting fire in the hearth. He adopts contentment as a dead person does. He gets fruit by living near the Guru as the silk-cotton tree does by being near the sandalwood tree. Sikhs loving the Guru make their wisdom complete.

(A recent translator and commentator on the writings of Bhai Gurdas follows the phrase 'grinds flour' with a parenthesis 'for langar'. The silk-cotton tree growing near a sandalwood tree imbibes the tree's fragrance.)

Social Justice

The image which many outsiders have of Sikhs is one of military prowess or militancy. This is not the place to discuss the battles fought by Guru Gobind Singh or the eighteenth-century struggle for survival which resulted in the empire of Maharajah Ranjit Singh. Even less should we comment on the troubles of the 1980s which have so influenced the Sikh psyche. What, however, must be said is that social justice has always been important. The B40 Janam Sakhi suggests that Guru Nanak witnessed the sacking of Saidpur by the armies of Babur and contains the story of a meeting with the emperor. A gurdwara near the city of Eminabad, which stands on the site of the old town, commemorates the place where Guru and conqueror met (see McLeod, B40 Janam Sakhi, p. 70). Whatever one's view of the historicity of the meeting, the Guru Granth Sahib does contain material known as the Babur bani (pp. 417-18). In these verses a terrible portrait is painted of women being raped by soldiers who did not bother to discriminate between the Hindus and Muslims who were in their path: Some lost their five times of prayer, some the time of puja' (AG 417).

The Babur bani has to do with the fate of the sufferers being determined by God:

> When they heard of the invasion of Emperor Babur millions of religious leaders failed to halt him ...No Mughal became blind and no one wrought any miracle... The Mughals aimed and fired their guns and the Pathans attacked with their elephants. Those whose letter has been torn in God's Court must die, my brothers... The Creator acts and causes others to act. To whom should we complain? Weal and woe are according to your will. To whom should one go to lament? The commander is pleased issuing God's commands. Nanak the mortal obtains what is destined for him. (AG 418)

In the Janam Sakhi the importance of the material which centres upon Babur and Saidpur is the light which it throws upon the Guru's concern for justice. The invading emperor is told: 'If you desire mercy [from God], release the prisoners.' Babur then clothed the captives and sets them free (McLeod, B40 Janam Sakhi, p. 78).

Whatever the historical basis of this narrative, and Bhai Gurdas too mentions a meeting (Var 26, Pauri 21), it is interpreted as a concern for human rights and social justice. When, in 1675, Guru Tegh Bahadur was martyred for responding to an appeal from a group of

Kashmiri Brahmins that he should ask the emperor of the time, Aurangzeb, to allow them religious freedom, he was following in a path deemed to be blazed by Guru Nanak.

Specific passages from the Guru Granth Sahib are cited in affirmation of God's concern for justice, for example:

> No one can enter the Court of Truth through falsehood. By telling nothing but lies, the Mansion is lost. (AG 146)

> Without the True One, the false do not attain the Divine Court. Being attached to avarice, the Mansion is lost. (AG 147)

> Everyone gathers in God's Court where one pen records all deeds. There, accounts are examined and evildoers shall be crushed like seeds in an oil press. (AG 143)

The scene in both verses is that of a court of justice. The simile in the third one is powerful, being taken from an everyday aspect with which most country dwellers would be familiar.

In a verse denouncing hypocrisy he says:

> You charge taxes for the cow and the Brahmin... You wear a mark on your forehead [tilak] and carry a jap mala but eat the food of the mleccha [unclean, non-Hindu]. In your home you perform puja, outside you read the kitaba [the scriptures of Islam] and adopt an Islamic lifestyle. Abandon hypocrisy. By practising Nam you will swim across. (AG 471)

One feels that here the Guru is not only being critical of those who suit their religiosity to the prevailing political situation, he is also concerned with oppression and the use of religion to despoil the poor by such things as taxing the animals on which they relied for sustenance. The ethical dimension is explicit, as in many other passages which attack religious duplicity, especially regarding caste.

Double standards of conduct, religious or social, suggest the reality of duality, something which the Gurus always denied. Their message was that in place of the four varnas there was one, that of humanity. Instead of four ashramas or stages of life, through which men (only) progressed, there was again one, that of the householder. The dharmas of the various zats were replaced by one, the universal calling to worship God through Nam and to perform sewa.

War and Peace

Guru Nanak clearly denounced the rapine that accompanied Babur's invasion of north India. Sometimes Sikh writers have claimed that he was a pacifist and that one of the developments of Sikhism was from a pacifist Panth to a militant Khalsa. This is perhaps too simple. Evidence for Sikh pacifism is lacking. *Ahimsa*, non-violence, an important concept among many Hindus, is not a part of Sikh teaching, though the Namdhari Sikh movement is largely pacifist. For the early Gurus taking a peace-war stance would scarcely have been possible. The Panth was too small to attract attention or to have much political voice. Guru Hargobind may have had a small standing army but it was his grandson, Guru Gobind Singh, who took the decisive step to found the Khalsa community. When he summoned them to assemble at Anandpur in 1699, he ordered them to come armed.

There are no grounds for claiming that Sikhism was ever a pacifist movement, but it did affirm the essential spirituality of all humanity and Guru Gobind Singh felt the need to justify going to war, especially against his nominal liege lord, the emperor. In a letter called Zafarnama, the Guru justified his actions and out of it comes a Sikh 'just war' theory. A couplet from it reads:

When all efforts to restore peace prove useless and no words avail,
Lawful is the flash of steel, it is right to draw the sword.

The five conditions for a righteous war (dharam yudh) are:

1. It should be a last resort when all other means have failed (as expressed in Zafarnama).
2. It should be waged without enmity or the desire for revenge. (Here one might be reminded of the desireless action, nish-kamakarma, which Arjuna was called upon to pursue by Krishna in the Bhagavad Gita.)
3. Territory should not be annexed but returned when hostilities have ended. Captured property should be given back. Looting and the taking of booty are forbidden.
4. The army should comprise only soldiers committed to the cause. There should be no use of mercenaries. It should act in a disciplined manner. The Rahit Namas of the Guru, the codes of conduct, should be adhered to strictly, such as no use of tobacco or alcohol, and no molesting of their adversaries' womenfolk.
5. Minimum force should be used, only sufficient to achieve the objective. This done, hostilities should cease.

These rules have always guided Sikhs, both in their military actions during the Mughal period, in the days of the Sikh Empire, and when they took part in the struggle for an independent India. A Sikh soldier must be a sant-sipahi, a 'saint-soldier', with the word sant coming first in order. The Sikh reputation for courage should never be allowed to overshadow the importance of spiritual principles. Though Sikhs have often been regarded as a warrior nation, especially by the British, many Sikhs have adopted a policy of non-violence in the pursuit of justice, as the Christian missionary, C. F. Andrews observed. In 1921, during the gurdwara reform movement when Sikhs were claiming the control of gurdwaras from private owners who had been granted possession by the British, Sikh reformers staged a non-violent protest at the Guru Ka Bagh gurdwara near Amritsar. They were met by force from policemen led by two English officers. The Sikhs faced them silently, their hands placed together in prayer. One Englishman felled a Sikh using his brass-tipped lathi. The demonstrator scrambled to his feet only to be knocked down again. The same treatment was meted out to the other Sikhs by the officers or their men. This was not a unique example of Sikh use of non-violence. It and similar incidents involving Hindus, Muslims, and Sikhs were eventually responsible for ending British rule.

When these regulations are considered in the context of normal acts of war in the subcontinent or elsewhere for that matter, their human concern is remarkable.

Ecology

This a feature of ethics that is only now coming into prominence. In 2001 it was the subject of a conference in Chandigarh and the Satguru of the Namdhari Sikhs has long been concerned about caring for the planet. So was the great humanitarian who established the Pingalwara in Amritsar to care for the sick and homeless who were often rejected by their families, Bhagat Puran Singh. He wrote tracts against government policies of deforestation and refused to accept state aid for his institution while such practices continued. The subject, however, is one that can be contentious. Punjabi farmers, in their successful efforts to produce high yields have used methods that have polluted river systems and had other harmful effects upon the population.

Amniocentesis

One of the uses of the modern medical procedure known as amniocentesis is that of discovering the sex of the foetus. Some Sikhs, and other groups, have followed the test by abortion should the child in the womb be female. This, of course, is contrary to the teachings of the Gurus regarding female infanticide. Another consequence of the practice is a decline in the number of females in the population. In the 2001 census there were 874 women per thousand men, in 1991 the ratio was 882 per thousand. Of course, there are no statistics of the incidence of abortion among different religious groups. Not all will be Sikhs, but some certainly are.

IVF

Artificial insemination of a woman with the sperm of a man who is not her husband is morally wrong. It can lead to all kinds of suspicion and place considerable stress upon a marriage, resulting often in divorce, something that brings great stigma onto a wife, especially. Perhaps for centuries, it has been the custom in Punjabi communities for a childless couple to adopt, albeit unofficially, nieces or nephews. This solution, however, is becoming increasingly impracticable as the size of families falls as the result of family planning.

Transplant Surgery

It has long been the custom for Sikh medical teams to go from the towns into the villages to treat people who are uncared for. Citing the examples of Guru Arjan and Guru Tegh Bahadur, Sikh humanitarians have encouraged families to donate the organs of dead members, sacrificing their lives as the martyr Gurus did for the needs of others.

Genetic Engineering

Sikhs believe that human life begins at conception. There is a view among many Sikhs that altering the genetic makeup of a foetus is interfering with nature. Sikhs have great respect for the natural form and believe it should not be tampered with. If a couple knows that there is a risk of passing on a genetic disorder they should use contraceptive means to avoid it. Some consultants, however, think that this scientific knowledge is God given and should be used to benefit humanity.

Khalsa Ethics

The Khalsa had at least two distinctive aspects to it. First, it was intended to recover the authority of the Guru. During the years prior to its institution, the masands had increased their influence.

Established to assist the Gurus in organising the Panth, they had become venal and independent. Second, there was a need to regulate such armed power that existed. Therefore, when Guru Gobind Singh created the Khalsa in 1699, he gave it a distinctive code of ethics and provided a 'just war' doctrine.

Most notable was the requirement to wear the symbolic uniform of the Khalsa, the five Ks at all times. The turban was not one of these, but male members were instructed to keep it.

Meat might be eaten, but not if it had been slaughtered according to Muslim custom. It must be killed by being beheaded with one sword blow. Taking drugs was strictly forbidden as was the consumption of alcohol and smoking tobacco. Adultery was also condemned. A Khalsa Sikh should only marry another Khalsa member. This was a sensible instruction since they should rise early in the morning, in the hour before dawn, and, during the day recite the five banis specified. One can scarcely imagine the family conflicts that would arise had one of the partners cut his or her hair and not respected the five Ks or turban.

Particularly interesting is the rule concerning the remarriage of widows and the care of daughters: 'If a woman's husband has died, she may, if she so wishes, find a match suitable for her, and remarry …The remarriage may be solemnised in the same way as the Anand marriage.' (The Anand marriage is one conducted in the presence of the Guru Granth Sahib and strictly speaking the only form of marriage which Sikhs recognise.) It also decrees that 'A Sikh should not kill his daughter nor maintain any relations with a killer of a daughter' (p. 24; SGPC undated English version). Dowries and forced marriages were specifically condemned.

It can be seen that the Khalsa ethical code found in the Rahit Maryada has influenced Sikh ethics in general. However, for the Khalsa member the obligations are enforced by the Khalsa community. Failure to observe them incurs various penalties. Serious lapses, such as cutting the hair, or taking drugs, kurahits, would result in the offender being called an apostate, *patit*. Other members would have nothing to do with them socially, though they would be encouraged to continue to worship in the gurdwara and take karah parshad. No one has a right to exclude anyone else from the possibility of being influenced by God's grace. Should a patit repent they may be readmitted to the Khalsa by full initiation, but the Khalsa Panth would need to be assured of their sincerity. Minor offences, known as tankhahs, are punished by a requirement for the offender to clean the shoes of the sangat for example, or washing up after langar. Great care should be taken not to humiliate the member. Taking alcohol and dyeing the hair are examples of tankhahs.

The famous Sikh acclamation 'Raj Karega Khalsa' (translated as 'the Khalsa will rule, no enemy shall remain. All who endure suffering and privation shall be brought to the safety of the Guru's protection') is pronounced by the whole sangat at the conclusion of Ardas and can be interpreted in a number of ways. It has often been seen as the battlecry of the Khalsa army. It can also be understood as an affirmation that one day Sikhs will be supreme. There is also the potential for an ethical interpretation: the conduct that Khalsa members are required to embrace will become that of the whole Panth, and humanity. The reign of the Khalsa is, in effect, the universal reign of God, a time when all humankind will live in safety and bliss.

10

Sikh Family Life

Sikhism is very much a family religion. The concept of the extended family is one that anyone who studies Sikhism should be aware of. Let one anecdote illustrate its value. A Sikh died leaving a wife, two sons and five daughters. The eldest son found work to put his younger brother through college. When he had graduated, the older brother went to university. Then the two men arranged the marriages of their sisters, the eldest first, then their own. The younger brother took their mother into his home.

Caste

What westerners term 'caste' is endemic to the Indo-Pakistan-Bangladeshi subcontinent. The inclusion of Pakistan may seem surprising, but society, especially rural society, is dominated by certain groups, Rajputs and Jats in particular. Rajputs are the traditional political leaders, Jats small landowners or peasants. Beneath them come many groups, or biradaris, independent of one another but owing allegiance to the main groups and economically and social dependent. Britons who went to India with the East India Company were encouraged in the seventeenth century to marry Indian women. When the policy was reversed a large number of Anglo-Indians faced an uncertain future. Many of them found work with the newly developing railways and have formed a virtual caste of their own, marrying among themselves and remaining distinct in their way of life. Christians have enjoyed a similar experience, being shunned by other groups and divided among themselves. For example, a Brahmin convert fell in love with another Brahmin Christian. His family was opposed to their marriage until they discovered that she did not even eat eggs as part of her vegetarian diet, that meant she was of superior status to them so she was an acceptable match for their son. Rural Christians seldom marry into groups other than their own. Dalits (the word means oppressed), who are even outside the caste system's social order, seldom gain preferment to the position of bishop. It has been known for Christians from the higher castes to take communion before Dalits so that they would not be polluted by touching and drinking from a vessel used by their inferiors. There is no need to develop this theme further; the point has, hopefully, been made that to be a member of subcontinental society is to be caught up in the caste system. It would be extraordinary if Sikhs were the one community to be free from it.

The origins of caste need not concern us. At its simplest it is both religious and social, though to draw a distinction is probably not something that Indians might recognise. Those who think of it in only social terms, however, forget or ignore the fact that ritual pollution, an aspect of religion, is part of it. Pollution is not confined to India and Hinduism, of course. The churching of women after childbirth in some Christian denominations can reflect the fact that the process of conceiving and bearing a child is polluting. So can the emphasis upon celibacy. A chancel rail beyond which those who are not specially ordained may pass can have a similar significance. Muslims consider dogs ritually impure; the opposition to them being used to sniff out drugs on Iranian airliners is not merely anger against their innocence being impugned. Nor is the washing of hands before handling the Qur'an and Wudu before prayers. A high-caste Hindu family may employ a servant to wash cooking utensils, but they will then run water over them to remove taint resulting from the servant's touch before using them.

In practice the jati system is likely to be more important than the varnashramadharma. It is possible to discover many Hindus who are unaware of their varna, unless they are Brahmins, or Shudras and Dalits who are not allowed to forget their status. Jati is an exogamous caste grouping, usually occupational. It has subdivisions known as gotras. Sikhs use the Punjabi terms zat, for the Hindi jati, and got for gotra. They will be used in this section.

Zat can have its positive side. In village India if the son of a potter were to marry the daughter of a barber she would bring with her no skills that could be used in the business of the family into which she was moving. She would not know how to throw a pot or prepare the clay, or paint the finished product. She would be useless within her new family and might even be unenthusiastic about her new way of life. Much better to find someone in one's own occupational group. Objections to zat are justified when it is discriminatory – when one group claims to be superior to another, socially and ritually.

Caste among Sikhs

The Gurus were primarily preachers of spiritual liberation. As they became responsible for an increasing number of followers, they addressed a variety of social concerns, though some always received their attention. For example, women were admitted to the Panth, and langar affirmed the ritual and social equality of everyone. In fact, ritual impurity was something that the Gurus vigorously denied. Guru Nanak said:

> All impurity contracted by touch is superstitious. Birth and death are by God's will, according to which we come and go. All food and drink is pure; for God has blessed them for our sustenance. Those who have realised this truth, through God, the Guru, do not believe in this kind of impurity. (AG 472)

and

> If the mind is unclean, it cannot be purified by worshipping stones, visiting holy places, living in forests, and wandering around as ascetics. (AG 586)

The predominant importance of zat and got is in the area of marriage. They should be within the zat, but traditionally Sikhs look at the family or got name of their grandparents and avoid marrying a partner who shares one of their names. Thus a Virdi will not marry a Virdi, a Sond a Sond, or a Patel a Patel, for example. This rule may not always be followed strictly. Nevertheless, there is a strong tendency to marry within one's zat. Thus Jat marries Jat and Khatri marries Khatri.

Guru Nanak had as little place for the varnashramadharma as for ritual pollution. For him there was only one class, humanity, and this included everyone, woman as well as man. The four stages of life were summed up in one, that of grihastha or gristhi, the householder, which included all the rest. The family is at the core of Sikhism. Ideally the Sikh is a family person. There are, of course, unmarried Sikhs but parents seldom rest easy until their children are married, and have made them grandparents! As for the goals of life, there is only one, moksha or mukti, which entails the service (sewa) of others regardless of caste, religion or gender. All others are subsumed in it.

The Panth is not a caste-free community. Sometimes the question is asked why were all ten Gurus Khatris, though they did not all come from the same subgroup? The answer can only be conjectured. One reason may be the wish to create social coherence. We have seen that there was rivalry whenever the position of Guru fell vacant. Some stability came from the fact that all the Gurus came from the same group. It must also be remembered that caste has never become extinct, though the efforts of Mahatma Gandhi and others have reduced its divisiveness. The Gurus did implement policies aimed at reducing the importance of caste and it can be claimed that they laid the basis for a casteless society; worship was inclusive, women were accorded respect, langar required commensality, a practice that must have deterred many Brahmins from joining the Panth. The use of Kaur and Singh by the tenth Guru had the potential for rendering caste insignificant by providing the opportunity not to use zat or got names. Some Sikhs do, in fact, call themselves Mr Singh or Mrs Kaur, refusing to use got identity. It may be argued that the truly liberated Sikh will have no place for distinctions of caste.

Ritual Pollution

The notion of ritual pollution may be fairly uncommon; some people of higher caste will change their clothes and take a bath if they have been to the home of a Dalit, but such responses are rare, though in the nature of things difficult to quantify. Generally, within the Panth ritual pollution is not strongly regarded. Sikhs must worship together and share langar. Behind the closed door of the family home things may, however, be different.

Social Distinctions

On the other hand, social distinctions are more frequently maintained. Jats are landowners, Sikh, Hindu or, in Pakistan, Muslim. Ramgarhias are craftsmen, regarded as inferior by Jats because of their lack of land. Another group are Bhatras, relatively small in number but significant in such a country as the United Kingdom where they were often the first migrants. They are peddlers and traders traditionally and sold brushes, tins of polish and other small items from door to door in the 1920s. In Britain one may find Jat, Ramgarhia, or Bhatra gurdwaras, testimonies to zat separation. It is also common to find a Sikh using the got name by which the zat may be identified, sometimes together with Kaur or Singh, as, for example, Jaswant Singh Dhillon, Charanjit Kaur Sond. Seeing a K or S between a given name and the got may be a clue to identifying a Sikh as opposed to a Hindu; for example, Jaswant K Dhillon.

It is easy to be judgemental about caste. In response, two points at least must be made. First, there are many Sikhs who have rejected it and are known only as Jaswant Singh or Baljit Kaur. Second, Indian society is not individualistic as western society increasingly is. A daughter being gay or a son divorced may no longer bring reproach upon the whole family but the chances are that it will. In India if a Brahmin falls in love with and decides to marry a Dalit, it can and probably will affect the whole extended family. No one will want to marry their son or daughter to a family with such a reputation. Better to marry a Jat Hindu than for a Jat Sikh to marry a Sikh chamar. Family pride or honour, izzat, is a concept essential for the student of Indian religions to understand.

The Sikh family

Asceticism and celibacy are not regarded as virtues. The four varnas, the ashramas, stages of life, and dharmas, the legitimate pursuits of wealth, pleasure, love, and spiritual liberation, may be followed concurrently and are all included in the community of one humanity united to one God, the Panth. When Guru Nanak said:

> Contemplation of the True One brings liberation which enables one to be detached even in the midst of evil. Such is the distinctive greatness of the True Guru through whose grace and guidance one can attain liberation even while surrounded by wife and children. (AG 661)

His stress was not on 'even', as though a family was an irksome encumbrance; still less was he suggesting that it was 'evil', rather he was encouraging the Sikh to find liberation in the normal aspects of life.

Contrary to the way of world renunciation chosen by some Hindus, he advised:

> Remain in towns and near the main highways, but be alert. Do not covet your neighbour's possessions. Without Nam [God], we cannot attain inner peace or still our inner hunger. The Guru has shown me that all the life of the city, the real life of its shops, it is the inner life. We must be traders in truth, moderate in our eating and sleeping. (AG 939)

Moderation is a fundamental Sikh attitude to life.

Family Ceremonies

There are three family ceremonies, not including birthdays, which are not as often celebrated in India as in some Diaspora countries, and such events as graduation. The three are naming, marriage, and death. In addition, there will be a turban ceremony for sons, and often a birth ceremony in the home.

Birth ceremony

There is no formal ceremony associated with a child's birth, though parents will often give boxes of sweets or other confectionery to friends and relatives will visit the home bringing gifts, especially if the child is a boy. (In the Diaspora especially there is now more gender parity, but because of the importance of sons in Punjabi culture more fuss may still be made of boys. This, of course, is not something peculiar to Sikhs.)

The birth of the child is normally marked by a respected member of the community visiting the home, and five people pouring some water into a small metal bowl to which some sugar is added and stirred in while reciting the first five verses of Guru Nanak's Japji. A few drops of the sanctified water, amrit, are then poured into the baby's mouth, the rest is given to the mother.

Sometimes, if this ceremony has not taken place in the home, the parents will take their baby to the gurdwara where s/he will be placed before the Guru Granth Sahib and then given some honey on the tip of a kirpan.

Naming

In Punjab, the baby, who may already have been given a pet name such as Rani or Dolly, which will be widely used in the family circle, will be taken to the gurdwara to be given a name. The timing of the occasion will be convenient to the community. In the Diaspora the baby may be taken to the gurdwara on the way home after leaving the hospital. Otherwise it may be taken on a Sunday, the normal occasion for diwan. The mother will proudly carry the baby, especially if it is her first and a son; the father may bring some coverings called rumalas to place on the Guru Granth Sahib. All close family members will take part in these practices. The family will also offer karah parshad, made at home, both in India and the Diaspora. The congregation will sing:

> I have the support of God, the almighty, so my sufferings and sorrows are over. Men and women alike, rejoice. God has been good to everyone. O devotees of God, there is peace all over because God's love has spread everywhere. (AG 628)

The new member of the sangat is welcomed with this hymn:

> God has been kind to me. The almighty one has fulfilled my longing. I have come home purified by God's love and obtained blessing, happiness and peace. O saintly people, only God's Name can give us true liberty. Always remember God and keep doing good, day and night. (AG 621-22)

As they sing this hymn the parents promise to bring up their child as a Sikh so that one day, as an adult, he or she can make their own personal commitment to God.

Another popular hymn is a verse that the mother of Guru Arjan composed when he was born:

> Dear son, this is your mother's blessing. May God never be out of your mind even for a moment. Meditation on God should be your constant concern. It purges people from all faults. May God, the Guru, be kind to you. May you love the company of God's people. May God robe you with honour and may your food be the singing of God's praises. (AG 496)

A member of the congregation faces the scripture and recites Ardas. The granthi will ask the parents to lay the child on the floor in front of the Guru Granth Sahib and will then open the Book at random and read the first verse on the left-hand page. The initial letter of this word will provide the initial letter of the child's name. When the family has chosen it, the granthi will announce it in a clear voice: 'Jaswant Kaur' or 'Jaswant Singh'. To show its approval the sangat will shout: 'Jo bole so nihal', a traditional cry that cannot be translated satisfactorily. Six verses of the Anand Sahib are then chanted and Ardas concludes the ceremony.

Most given names can be used of girls and boys. The only way of distinguishing the gender may be to look at the initial that follows: Jaswant K. Sohel will be female, Jaswant S. Sohel, a male.

In the 1960s some British Sikh women training as nurses, found the Kaur/Singh use of names a cause of confusion and embarrassment. The trainee might be registered as Amrit Singh, after all 'Singh' would be the father's name on the birth certificate, but upon completing her course she might say that her real Sikh name was Amrit Kaur. If she wished to be registered with her real name she would have to begin her training again. The matter has now been settled by the British Nursing Council, so one is unlikely any more to meet a young Sikh lady who tells you she is Nurse Singh!

Naming Converts

Fully to assume Sikh identity, a convert should undertake amrit initiation. The naming ceremony will be incorporated into this.

Marriage

For a marriage to be acceptable it is essential that many members of the two families assent to it. Arranged marriages are still the norm, especially in India where customs are slowest to change. A number of injunctions are laid upon Sikhs: the couple must agree to the arrangement, forced marriages are against the Sikh code of ethics; child marriages are forbidden. The Gurus frowned upon the dowry system and the Indian government has outlawed it, but it still features strongly in family discussions, as may the bride's ability to enable her husband to emigrate to North America or the UK. The most important issue, as has already been stated, is usually zat, even though strict Sikh teaching is that it should not be a consideration.

The importance of family is demonstrated in the ceremony of milni. The groom's party will be welcomed by the bride's family and gifts will be formally exchanged, father to father, brother to brother, uncle to uncle, in accordance with their status in their respective families. Then they will be welcomed with food and drink. The womenfolk will have observed milni separately, mother exchanging gifts with mother and sisters with sisters, for example.

The marriage ceremony

For a Sikh marriage to be acceptable it is only necessary that it should take place in the presence of the Guru Granth Sahib. Should legal requirements demand a civil ceremony this may be held at any time before the gurdwara wedding or at the beginning of it. Weddings are often solemnised in gurdwaras in the Diaspora, but a large hall, a garden, even the roof of a Punjabi house may be chosen; if so, the Guru Granth Sahib will be ceremonially carried to it.

Relatives and guests will bow towards the Book and then sit on the floor. Men and women would always sit separately, but it is becoming more common for families to sit together. The groom's place is directly in front of the scripture.

Eventually the bride with a companion, often a female relative, takes her place at his left side. The person conducting the ceremony asks the couple and their parents to stand as s/he leads the congregation in prayer invoking God's blessing on the occasion. An appropriate scripture passage is read and the couple are reminded of their duties to one another as husband and wife. They are asked if they will fulfil their responsibilities faithfully and when they nod assent the end of the groom's scarf, pulla, is placed in the bride's right hand. They then stand to listen to the first verse of *Lavan* (which means encircling).

The four stanzas of Lavan, the wedding hymn composed by Guru Ram Das, read verse by verse as follows:

> By the first circling the Guru has shown the duties of the householder life. Sing the bani instead of the Vedas and hold fast to the faith which they reveal so that God may free you

from all evil inclinations. Cling to righteousness and contemplate God's Name, the theme of all scriptures. Devote yourself to the True Guru and all evil will depart. Those minds are indeed blessed which are filled with the sweetness of the Name. To them bliss comes effortlessly.

In the second circling you are to recognise that God has caused you to meet the True Guru who washes away the self-centredness of those who sing God's praises. I stand reverently face to face with the Guru. God is the soul of the universe, the only One, being within us and outside us. There is nothing which God does not pervade. Songs of rejoicing are heard in the company of the godly. Slave Nanak says, in the second round divine music is heard.

In the third circling longing for God and detachment from the world wells up. By our good fortune, in godly company, we encounter God whose purity is found through singing divine praises. Good fortune has brought us into the fellowship of the saints in which the story of the ineffable One is told. God's love fills our minds and absorbs us, as we have been blessed with a good destiny which is recorded on our foreheads. In the third circling, says Nanak, God's love is awakened in the heart.

In the fourth round the mind attains Divine Knowledge and union with God becomes complete. This blissful state is reached through the Guru's grace. The sweetness of the beloved pervades our souls and bodies. God is dear to me and I to God on whom my mind is fixed day and night. By exalting God I have achieved my heart's desire. The beloved [God] has completed the union. The bride's mind has blossomed with the beloved's name. The beloved is united with the holy bride. Says slave Nanak, in the fourth round I have become one with the One. (AG 773-74)

At the end of each verse the couple circle the scripture in a clockwise direction, the groom leading, while the musicians sing the stanza which has just been read. With the conclusion of the fourth circling, the couple are married. The prayer Ardas will now be offered and will include a request for God's blessing upon the newly married couple and their families.

Lavan uses the union of man and woman to describe the relationship of God and devotee. Awe, love, restraint, and harmony are the four steps outlined by its composer, Guru Ram Das. They apply equally to the spiritual life and to the marital relationship.

After the ceremony gifts are given: a coconut from the bride's mother, coins and notes, some of which will be pinned to the groom's shirt, and garlands of bank notes, while others join the coconut in the pulla. Bride and groom will also be garlanded. Speeches and specially composed poems and songs may be read or sung.

Sikh weddings should be held in the morning, with noon now becoming a deadline for the beginning of the ceremony. There should be no consideration given to auspicious days or seasons. The couple will eventually go to the bride's home from which they will depart for her husband's. This ceremonial departure is known as dohli. The next day she returns to her parental home and may stay for a week before her husband comes for her and they go away to begin their life together. The western custom of the honeymoon is acquiring some popularity in the Diaspora.

Funerals

When someone is dying relatives and friends will gather at the bedside to recite the Sukhmani, the beautiful psalm of peace composed by Guru Arjan.

Death should not be marked by grieving and loud wailing, after all, hopefully, the dead person is going to enjoy the fullness of union with God. In reality bereavement does, of course, bring tears and a sense of loneliness; however, at all times a Sikh should be *chardhi kala*, literally, 'in high spirits', that is cheerful.

In India the body would be cremated on the day of death so long as this can be done decorously before sundown, otherwise it will be postponed till the next morning.

Tender loving care is provided by the family not the nursing staff in many Indian hospitals. They will camp in the grounds and stay with the patient through much of the day. They will prepare food at meal times. The professional nursing staff is there to provide the medical services which they have been trained to give. It has come as a surprise to visitors to Britons from the subcontinent to discover that sometimes strict rules for visiting hours are enforced, that a patient may only have two visitors at a time, and that s/he is expected to eat food prepared in the hospital canteen. Of course, members of the third and fourth generation are accustomed to this, having probably experienced it as children or at the birth of a child. They may well be unaware of hospital regime of their ancestral homeland. For elderly people in the Asian communities their first hospitalisation can be a more than usually traumatic experience.

Should death be the end of the medical process, families expect to be with the person who is dying and to remain with the body for sometime after death. To be removed while last attempts are made to maintain life only to be informed that they have been unsuccessful and the loved one is dead can make the family feel that they have failed in their duty. Sikhs should gather at the bedside to console themselves and the departing soul by reading verses from the scriptures, especially Sukhmani. It gives the assurance that anyone who meditated sincerely upon God's name will not suffer rebirth but live eternally with God.

Postmortems are greatly disliked by Sikhs. They seem to be a violation of the body of a loved one and they prevent funeral preparations being made.

Funeral Rites
A line of the Guru Granth states: 'The dawn of a new day is the herald of a sunset. Earth is not your permanent home' (AG 793). This is a message that Sikhs should always bear in mind. The beautiful hymn Sohila, which Sikhs should use in their evening devotions, sets out the aims of life as follows:

> Know the real purpose of being here, gather up treasure under the True Guru's guidance. Make your mind God's home. If God abides with you undisturbed, you will not be reborn (AG 13).

The evidence for a life beyond the present one lies for the Sikh in such assurances as these, in the belief that the Gurus were themselves living in the divine presence when they were commanded to resume a human form to preach God's message to humanity, and in personal experience. Some people become jiva mukt, that is they attain liberation while still in their human bodies. This would be considered the logical conclusion of the Gurus' emphasis upon God as immanent. Sikhs would speak of a relationship with God which they could not envisage as ending at physical death. God's love is eternal; life beyond this earthly existence is regarded as becoming merged in the Divine rather than a personal resurrection. In fact, resurrection and an end of the historical process do not feature strongly, if at all, in Sikh thought.

Funeral services should proclaim the hope and promise of eternal life. Sikhs tend to prepare the body themselves and dress it in the five Ks. This is done in many areas of the Diaspora by arrangement with a firm of undertakers who have become accustomed over the years to conducting Sikh funerals.

In rural Punjab 'Waheguru' will be repeated and hymns will be sung as the procession walks to the cremation ground. In the West these are chanted at home and in the gurdwaras by the congregation. The coffin will remain open so that last respects may be paid. The

Sikh Code of Conduct lays down the order of service, which should therefore be the same in general terms throughout the world:

> The dead body is washed and clothed (complete with the five symbols) before it is taken out on a bier to the cremation ground. The procession starts after a prayer and suitable hymns from the Guru Granth Sahib are sung on the way. At the cremation ground the body is placed on the pyre. Ardas is recited and the nearest relative will light the pyre; usually this will be the eldest son. When the pyre is fully ablaze, someone reads Sohila and offers prayers for the benefit of the dead. Then the people come away and leave the relatives of the deceased at their door, where they are thanked before departing. (pp. 17-18)

In Britain and elsewhere where there are public crematoria, the essentials of this instruction are observed though a hearse and private cars or hired buses are used. Male relatives will formally help to put the coffin in the incinerator.

After the funeral Sikhs may return to the gurdwara. The funeral is unlikely to take place on the day the Sikh dies, or the next day, in the Diaspora. Relatives from India, Singapore, or other distant locations must be given time to make their journeys.

Disposal of the dead

Guru Nanak was asked whether the Hindu custom of cremation or the Islamic method, inhumation, was correct. He refused to enter into the controversy but did humorously point out that the best clay for making pots seemed to be found in cemeteries, implying that there was a chance that the decomposed body ended up by being burned! (AG 466). There was a continuing argument among his followers as the story is told that when the Guru was dying those who came from a Hindu background asked for permission to cremate him, while the Muslim devotees wished to bury him. Guru Nanak told them to cover his body in a cloth and place flowers by it: Hindu one side, Muslim the other. Those whose flowers remained fresh might dispose of the corpse as they wished. In the morning they found both groups of flowers still fresh but the body had gone! The Guru was indifferent to how the body should be dealt with. The only thing that mattered was the state of the soul. If it had not achieved liberation its prospects were bleak indeed. In fact, Sikhs today tend accept the customs of the land in which they live. For choice they cremate, but in Arab countries, where this is not possible, they may bury their dead – though some may fly the body back to Punjab.

British Sikhs sometimes arrange for the ashes of their dead relatives to be taken out to sea and thrown into the water while prayers are said. In India, the Ganges at Hardwar or Kiratpur on the Sutlej are popular sites for disposing of ashes.

The Khalsa Code of Discipline forbids 'the erection of monuments over the remains of the dead' (p. 17). Samadhis, built over the remains of devout men and women, encourage practices which Sikhs regard as superstitious.

Many families organise a sidharan path, a reading of the Guru Granth Sahib that should be completed within ten days. Family members may gather in the evening after work to participate in it. If the person who died was a male head of family, the after-death ceremonies will include tying the turban of his successor in the presence of the family.

Turban Tying

Besides designating the head of a family, turban tying takes place when a young boy of about nine to twelve years of age is able to tie his own turban. There will be a family celebration that may or may not include a religious element. Although the wearing of a turban is most important in the lives of Sikhs who keep the uncut hair or belong to the Khalsa, the ceremony may be celebrated in homes where the men cut their hair. From the day that it has been adopted the boy should always wear it. There is sometimes concern in the Diaspora when a boy goes home on a Friday with his hair in plaits only to return on Monday with it covered by a turban. Head teachers or principals may feel that their authority is being threatened! When they are invited to the ceremony such fears can be allayed.

Turban tying is an important ceremony after the death of a family head in order publicly to affirm who has taken his place.

To strike a Sikh on the head, knocking off his turban, is one of the greatest insults that one can commit!

Some Proverbs

Much can be learned about a culture from its sayings. Here are a few popular ones that illustrate the importance of the family.

> Sorrow for a dead father lasts for six months.
> Sorrow for a dead mother lasts for a year.
> Sorrow for a dead wife lasts until a second wife arrives.
> Sorrow for a dead son lasts forever.

A good son is the light of a family.

A woman who has a daughter sits in a chair. One who has sons leans against the wall.

From a debt to one's father, from a single daughter, and from travelling a mile alone, may God preserve you.

You have a future life when your grandson plays at the door.

Fall from a horse and you may be saved. Fall from self-respect and you are lost.

Modesty is the embellishment of women.

A family survives by having one head.

11

Initiation

Initiation (also known as amrit pahul, amrit sanskar or khande ka pahul) is the one specifically religious rite undertaken by individuals. Sometimes it is described as a sacrament or even baptism, but care must be taken in using these terms when communicating with people who are of a different faith. They are best avoided. (It can be almost as misleading as calling a granthi a priest as has already been mentioned.)

Strictly speaking, it is not birth that makes a Sikh, but illumination and consequently a way of life which Bhai Gurdas defined thus:

> Dead to the world, a Sikh lives in the spirit of the Guru. One does not become a Sikh by merely paying lip service. A Sikh dispels all doubts and fears and lives a life of deep patience and faith, being truly a living sacrifice, God's loving slave.
>
> Doing what God wills Sikhs forget hunger and sleep in their love. Their hands are busy helping the needy and comforting the weary, and busy washing their feet. Magnanimous, tolerant, and serene they live to serve humanity.
>
> In glory Sikhs do not laugh. In suffering they do not weep. They are seers living in God's presence, devotees imbued with love. They steadily grow into perfection and are blessed and adored like the new moon on the Muslim day of Eid. (Var 3, Pauri 18)

Until 1699 initiation was by charn amrit. Literally this can be translated as foot-nectar and was prepared by pouring water over the Guru's feet and catching it in a bowl. The nectar was then drunk by those receiving initiation. The Indian practice of showing respect to a person by clasping or kissing his feet is very ancient. Touching the feet of a saintly person is considered to be a way of receiving a blessing. Bhai Gurdas wrote of Guru Nanak:

> He initiated his disciples with charn amrit, water sanctified by the touch of his lotus feet, and gave a new code of conduct as the highway to the path of truth. (Var 23)

From an examination of the Vars, spiritual and moral injunctions were laid upon initiated Sikhs. They were to bathe daily early in the morning and then spend time in meditation; to treasure seeing the Guru (darshan) and being given opportunities to touch his feet, but more important was obedience to his teaching. They were to read the gurbani with understanding and preach it. Presumably this is the origin of Sikh concern for literacy and education: to see the Guru and hear him was not enough, they should be able to read his hymns and be sufficiently conversant with the faith in order to be able to communicate it to others. At this time, in the early seventeenth century, Sikhism would seem to have been a missionary faith.

The form of initiation changed in 1699. The normal Vaisakhi assembly took place at Anandpur. The date was 30 March by European reckoning because the Gregorian calendar had not yet been introduced. The precise events of that Vaisakhi day may now be uncertain. It has been suggested that the Code of Discipline attributed to that occasion evolved during the eighteenth and early nineteenth centuries What concerns us here is not rehearsal or evaluation of this evidence but an attempt to explain the significance of the *khande ka pahul* ceremony of initiation. We shall therefore examine the rite as it is performed today after a brief summary of what is traditionally agreed to have happened on the first occasion.

Vaisakhi 1699

When Guru Gobind Das, or Gobind Rai as he is sometimes called, summoned his Sikhs to assemble before him as usual at Anandpur for the Vaisakhi mela, he instructed them to come armed. These were difficult and dangerous times; Sikhs stress the Islamisation policy of Aurangzeb. The Mughal Emperor had imposed the jizya and replaced mandirs and gurdwaras with mosques. His most zealous servants encouraged forced conversions, even though Sura 2:256 of the Qur'an affirms that 'there can be no compulsion in religion'.

The Guru, dressed in saffron, came out of his tent and addressed his Sikhs telling them that they must be prepared to give their lives for the faith. He emphasised this by asking for a Sikh to come forward who was willing to give his head for the Guru. Eventually, Daya Ram, a Kshatriya, came forward and was taken into the tent. There was a thud and then the Guru reappeared, blood-stained sword in his hand. He sought a second volunteer. Some Sikhs fearfully left the gathering. After some time a Delhi Jat responded. He too was led into the tent. A washerman, Mukham Das, from Dwarka in Gujerat, next obeyed the summons. Then followed Sahib Chand, a Bihari barber. When a fifth

Sikh Himmat Rai, a potter from Jagganath in Orissa, was led into the tent, the Guru asked for no more affirmations of obedience but brought out all five men clothed as he was in a saffron robe tied at the waist by a blue sash and wearing a turban. All were unharmed. It is idle to speculate upon what actually happened inside the tent. It only detracts from the significance of the event, namely the willingness of Sikhs to give complete loyalty to their Guru. Their unity was symbolised and stressed by each dressing alike and taking a common name, Singh, lion. The Guru became Gobind Singh.

The five men were initiated into a new community, the Khalsa. The word was used by Mughal Emperors to designate the land that was their personal property. A further symbolic sign. Initiation was by water being put into a bowl, sugar crystals were added provided by the Guru's wife, Mata Jeeto – a polluting act for anyone who held such un-Sikh views. It was then given to the initiates to drink and poured over their heads. Guru Gobind Singh himself became the sixth Khalsa member, initiated by the other five. The call was given for other Sikhs to come forward. It is said that twenty thousand men responded. The Khalsa became the core of Sikh resistance to all violent threats to the Panth's existence.

The Initiation Ceremony Today

Nowadays, initiation may take place at any time of year, though Vaisakhi is a popular season. Strictly speaking the initiates should be over fourteen years of age, but there is ample evidence of young children being initiated in Punjab. The rite is the same for Sikhs and non-Sikhs, but some Codes of Discipline require a three-year period as a catechumen before admission. The person who asks to become a Khalsa Sikh must be in possession of the five Ks, should be tidily dressed and be known to be attempting to follow the Sikh way of life as well as accepting the doctrines of Sikhism.

The five Ks are so called because in Punjabi each begins with the letter K. They are:

Kesha: Uncut hair. This symbolises the belief that a Sikh should not interfere with the natural God-given form. Circumcision, for example, is rejected. Sometimes hospitals will tell of cases where a Sikh was very reluctant to have any body hair shaved before an operation.

Kangha: This is a small comb worn in the hair to keep it tidy. It is a reminder of the stricture that cleanliness lies at the heart of the religion. Yogis and other devotees often had matted, unkempt hair. Sikhs should wash the hair regularly.

Kara: This steel wristlet is normally worn on the right hand. Perhaps it had a functional purpose at one time, to protect the sword arm. Now it affirms the oneness of God and the union of the wearer with God. It is sometimes described as God's handcuff, keeping the wearer attached to Waheguru. Sikhs will say that it helps keep them from doing wrong. Should one be tempted to steal, for example, the kara will remind the wearer of his or her moral responsibilities as a follower of the Guru.

Kirpan: The sword that Sikhs were told to wear when they attended the Guru in 1699 has also symbolic as well as practical significance. It is worn in devotion to truth and should only be drawn as a last resort in a righteous cause. At the amrit ceremony and on other occasions full-length swords are worn, but usually it will be of about twelve to twenty centimetres long and may be worn hanging by a shoulder strap underneath the shirt so as not to alarm anyone. It should never be described as a dagger, a weapon used by sinister assassins.

Kaccha: These shorts tied with a drawstring should, like the other Ks, be worn both by men and women. In Indian villages men may be seen wearing them as they work in the fields. Where western dress has been adopted they will constitute an undergarment. Modesty, especially relating to sex, is an extremely important virtue and this is the meaning behind the fifth K.

It will be noticed that the turban is not one of the five Ks. It is worn as a distinctive piece of Sikh apparel but not to keep the hair tidy. The Kangha does this – and baldheaded Sikhs will wear it even though it has no functional purpose!

The rite of initiation must be performed by five people, men or women, who re-enact the original ceremony. All five must possess the five Ks and be physically complete as well as devout members of the Khalsa community. Both outwardly and inwardly, they should represent the perfect human form. As long as the place where the ceremony is held is one where there is privacy, there is no restriction upon the location or on the numbers taking part. Lapsed Sikhs (patits) who have broken the Code of Discipline may undergo the ceremony a second or even a third time, though the sincerity of such a person would be seriously and severely questioned.

One of the five conducting the ceremony then explains the principles of the Sikh faith and asks those about to be initiated whether they accept them. A prayer for the preparation of amrit is offered and a sixth person, acting as granthi, reads a passage from the scriptures. The five (panj piare) kneel around an iron bowl (batta) on a pedestal (sonera) with their right knee on the ground and the left raised. They place sugar crystals (patasas) in the bowl and, one by one, stir it with a short double-edged sword (khanda) as they recite the Japji of Guru Nanak, the Jap and ten Swayyas of Guru Gobind Singh, the Chaupai, which is part of the evening hymn, and the first five and last stanzas of the Anand. These constitute an excellent precis of the Sikh faith as stated in the words of the Gurus. When the nectar is ready, the panj piare lift up the bowl and one of them offers another prayer.

During this impressive preparation the candidates have been sitting or standing while they listen to the gurbani, becoming more deeply and spiritually involved as the recitation proceeds. Now they come forward one by one and kneel in the same manner as the panj piare. Each one is asked to say 'Waheguru ji ka Khalsa, sri Waheguru ji ki fateh' ('The Khalsa is of God, the victory is to God') and then is given a handful of amrit to drink before nectar is sprinkled five times on their eyes and hair. Any amrit which is left is drunk by the initiates who sip it from the batta.

Repetition of the Mul Mantra five times by the panj piare, echoed on each occasion by the initiates, begins the third part of the ceremony. The senior member of the five then tells the new Khalsa members that they are children of the same family whose parents are Guru Gobind Singh and his wife, Mata Sahib Kaur. They must set aside all other religious beliefs and practices and cling only to the teachings of the Gurus.

The service ends with the Ardas, the reading of a randomly chosen passage from the Adi Granth, and the sharing of karah parshad which all initiates take from the same dish, symbolising unity and equality. Anyone who has come new to Sikhism will be given a name and take the Khalsa name of Kaur or Singh following the procedure for naming a child before karah parshad is distributed.

There is no age restriction relating to initiation. Sometimes a whole nuclear family will take amrit and this may include children who are not yet teenagers. Some Sikhs have been known to wait until middle age or beyond, feeling that they are not yet ready spiritually to follow the Khalsa Code.

12

The Sikh Calendar, Gurpurbs and Melas

Festivals and their meaning

Although every day should be regarded in the same way and there is no weekly holy day, or any notion that one day may be more auspicious than another, nevertheless Sikhs do observe some occasions known as gurpurbs and others, called melas or fairs. These are usually celebrated, however, at the weekend in countries where it is a period of rest from normal work. Elsewhere they decide on a convenient date. There has usually been no tendency to keep children away from school on the holy day in Britain, though Sikh schools in India may close or organise special celebrations as faith schools do in many countries. This attitude is likely to continue unless external pressures prompt (or perhaps provoke) Sikhs to behave differently. If, for example, other religions demand holidays so that they can observe certain occasions, local Sikhs might follow suit so as not to be outdone. Some British local authorities have an agreement that schools may be closed on such occasions as Guru Nanak's birthday or Diwali where the situation makes it desirable.

Sikhs have recently introduced a calendar dating from the birth of Guru Nanak in 1469. It is called the Nanakshahi Calendar and counts the birth year of Guru Nanak as year one. Early Sikh writings in the days before European influence naturally used the Samvat system and a few modern books retain it still as their authors attempt to distance themselves from the Raj!

The first use of festivals by Sikhs came in the time of Guru Amar Das who commanded his followers to assemble in his presence on the Hindu spring and autumn festivals, or melas, of Baisakhi, Diwali and Hola Mohalla. This was clearly a way of implementing his policy of developing a distinctive Sikh identity. People, at these times, had to choose where they belonged, with their Hindu kin or with the Guru. Festivals are important in forging and expressing identity, as some of the comments made above have implied, and this is what Guru Amar Das successfully did. The Sikh melas combine religious purpose and sheer festive enjoyment in the main places where they are observed.

Gurpurbs

The majority of Sikh festivals are gurpurbs, anniversaries of Gurus' birthdays and occasionally deaths, plus the anniversary of the first installation of the Adi Granth.

Sikhs celebrate them in the same way wherever they live. The main activity is a continuous reading of the Guru Granth Sahib, an akhand path, which is timed to take forty-eight hours and ends on the morning of the day when the gurpurb is being observed – usually a Sunday in the Diaspora, for reasons of convenience. (Occasionally, a gurdwara may keep the birthday of Guru Nanak in the very early morning as tradition records that he was born at that time on a moonlight night during the fragrant hour, which is the last watch of the night (i.e. the hours before dawn).) During an akhand path, readers work in relays with stints of no more than two hours at a time, with someone always ready to take over should the person reading be taken ill. There is no difficulty in finding readers unless a sangat is small and has few members who can read the Guru Granth Sahib with the correct intonation.

After a ceremony called bhog, which brings the akhand path to its close, the celebration will continue with lectures, sermons, kirtan, and sometimes the reading of specially composed poems on the subject of the Guru who is being celebrated, perhaps in the context of the normal Sunday service in Diaspora countries. Passers-by may be offered fruit. In India there is a tradition of Sikhs walking round the neighbourhood in the early morning reciting shabads. A feature of many gurpurbs is nagar kirtan, the processing of the Guru Granth Sahib around the neighbourhood, led by five men on horseback representing the panj piare. The float carrying the scripture will be followed by members of the Sikh community.

The Nanakshahi Calendar

Most books on Sikhism written in English use the Common Era calendar. Thus the birth of Guru Nanak is given as 1469. Sikh writers of his time and later used the Bikrami or Samvat Calendar, which originated some 56 years ahead of the Common Era. So Guru Nanak's birth will be given as S 1526. The Samvat/Bikrami Calendar is, of course, totally independent of the Gregorian Calendar, hence the fact that in one Common Era year Guru Gobind Singh's birthday can appear twice, and in another not at all.

In 2003 CE the Sikhs adopted a new calendar, the Nanakshahi. After some discussion, this has now been widely implemented by the

Panth and it is this calendar that will be used here. It is dated from the birth of Guru Nanak, so 2003 CE was N 535. The dates of the main celebrations are:

5 January: birth of Guru Gobind Singh

14 April: Vaisakhi mela

2 May: birth of Guru Arjan

16 June: martyrdom of Guru Arjan

1 September: installation of the Guru Granth Sahib

24 November: martyrdom of Guru Tegh Bahadur

The melas of Hola Mohalla and Diwali will continue to be dated according to the Bikrami Calendar.

The birthday of Guru Nanak is still likely to be celebrated in the month of Kattak/Kartik for some years to come. This is the date favoured by the Bala Janam Sakhi and popularised in the nineteenth century. To retain it is a matter of common sense, though one day it may be relocated to Vaisakhi. Especially in Diaspora communities, sending greetings cards has become popular, mostly among second and third-generation settlers.

13

Sikh Attitudes to Other Religions

The life of Guru Nanak, as already outlined, and the Bhagat Bani provide evidence of the rich variety of religious belief and practice that existed in northern India during his lifetime. Buddhism was extinct and Christianity had not yet penetrated the region but the many forms of Hinduism and the increasing influence of Sunni Islam were to be encountered daily. It would be surprising if Guru Nanak had not noticed them and reacted to them. The fact is that he and his successors did and paid them much attention. To understand Sikhism fully it is necessary to be conversant with his response to them. Any study of Sikh attitudes to other religions must begin with Guru Nanak.

It was common until very recently to describe Sikhism as syncretistic, a blend of Hinduism and Islam. Writers suggested that the Guru took the best from the two religions! We must ask what constitutes the best, what criteria of choice can be used. His affirmation of one God might be seen as Islamic, his attitude to women might be said to accord with some forms of Hindu bhakti, but with a greater study of these facets, it will be recognised that, though his monotheism may be similar to that of some Sufis, an Islamic origin does not seem satisfactory. As for the equality of women and men, he seems to go well beyond the norms of his day, and we have not addressed such issues as ritual pollution or the divisions in society which are to be found in Islam as well as in the Hindu caste system. Sikhism must be considered independently and recognised to be a distinctive revealed religion if there is to be any hope of understanding it and its relationship with other faiths.

The basis of Guru Nanak's attitudes to the religions he encountered is his concept of God and humanity. He had no human spiritual preceptor. Suggestions that he was a disciple of Kabir are based on unreliable sources.

Besides the belief that God is one, Guru Nanak taught that God had no garb, that is no form or attachments by which one could claim the deity to be Hindu or Muslim. He used Hari, Ram and Gopal, Allah, Khuda and Sahib (e.g. AG 903), depending on the beliefs of his hearers, but his fundamental affirmation was that 'My master is one, brother, the One who alone exists' (AG 350).

Guru Nanak was what might be described as a critical universalist, though taken to its logical limits, he might, perhaps, be said to hold a position which transcends accepting the authenticity or validity of all religions, for each, at some point, implies that the Truth is limited by or conditioned by its own tenets.

His acceptance of Islam may be seen from the following verses.

> There are five prayers, they have five names. The first is truthfulness, the second honest learning, the third charity in God's name, the fourth purity of intent, and the fifth God's admiration and praise. Repeat the kalima of good deeds [the statement that 'There is no God but God and Muhammad is his prophet'], then call yourself a prophet. (AG 141)

Of Allah he said:

> Baba Allah is inscrutable. He is boundless. His abode is holy and so are his names. He is the True Sustainer. His will surpasses comprehension. It cannot be described adequately. Not even a hundred poets assembled together could describe the smallest part of it. All hear and talk about him, none fully appreciates his worth. (AG 141)

> Allah consults no one when he makes or unmakes, gives or takes away. He alone knows his decree [qudrat], he alone is the doer. He beholds everyone and bestows grace on whom he wills. (AG 53)

These sentences might well have been uttered by a Muslim.

Guru Nanak could even find some place for the varna system and much more for the Vedas. He does not reject the Hindu varna structure, and certainly not the authenticity of the Vedas, as the following passages demonstrate:

> The way of union is the way of Divine Knowledge. With the Brahmin the way is through the Vedas, the Kshatriyas way is that of bravery. That of the Shudra is the service of others. The duty of all is meditation on the One. (AG 1353)

It should be noted that the Shudra has a spiritual duty, meditation, and this transcends the traditional socio-religious functions. Here the emphasis is not on purity but on service and Nam simran, the cardinal Sikh virtues.

> The Vedas preach the sermon of devotional service. He who continually hears and believes sees the Divine Light. The shastras and smirtis impress meditation on the Name. (AG 731, 832)

Hearing alone is not enough. Responding through faith is what matters:

> A fool residing with a pandit hears the Vedas and shastras.
> Like a dog with a crooked tail he remains unchanged. (AG 990)

Priestly domination of one group of people by another is anathema to Sikhs. Sometimes Guru Nanak criticised the potential for exploitation which resulted from religious power, whether it be of the Brahmin, yogi, or mullah. More fundamentally, he believed that the Nam-filled devotee, the gurmukh, had no need of the offices of such ministers or of intermediaries of any sort. Guru Nanak often spoke of the necessity of having a guru, but in doing so he was never commending himself but the Sat Guru, God.

Beyond the Vedas is their creator who must be attained if liberation is to be achieved: 'It is God who created the Vedas. It is through the One that the world is saved' (AG 930). Guru Nanak's primary belief in the immediacy of brahm vidya, the liberating knowledge of Brahman, meant that belief systems held a subordinate place in his theology. It does appear, however, that through aspects of them, such as imbibing the Vedic message or sincerely performing namaaz, God could be realised. We may not agree that conventional Hindu belief and Islam were fundamentally wrong. Truth could be reached through them, though it may be said to lie beyond them.

There is one religious tradition to which Guru Nanak refers with what might appear to be unwonted hostility. They appear to be beyond hope, though, as will be seen, that is not necessarily the whole story.

Jainism

Guru Nanak refers to Jains only twice in any detail. They have never been a numerically large, popular Indian way of liberation, but they were present in Punjab, in the Ambala district. The Jain movement is, in a sense, one with the Upanishads and Buddhism, but unlike the former, and in common with the way of the Buddha, it was regarded as unorthodox because it did not acknowledge the authority of the Vedas. It owes its origins to Mahavira, the twenty-fourth Tirthankara or teacher, who may have lived at about the same time as the Buddha, between 599 to 526 BCE as some writers suggest. Jainism is extremely austere and ethical in its teachings and requirements. The laity must take three vows – of non-violence, truthfulness and charity. This means that Jains are vegetarian, concerned for the environment, and have often practised as businessmen, such is their honesty. Such an austere religion has never appealed to the masses and today it may have less than four million adherents.

Jains do not believe in a personal creator God. Liberation is through their way of life and entails becoming a monk or nun; liberation may not be achieved in their present existence. It is non-theistic, the gods are themselves souls on the way to liberation. The religion is also dualistic, with a division into that which is alive (jiva), and that which is non-living (ajiva). Among the ajiva is karma, which attaches itself to the jiva and weighs it down, thus preventing the attainment of moksha, of mukti, to use the Sikh term. Jains were known to be in Lahore in the time of Emperor Akbar and wandered through Punjab in Guru Nanak's day. He certainly considered them deserving of attention and provides this unsympathetic description of them.

> They pluck the hairs from their heads, drink water in which people have washed, and beg leftovers. They rake up their excreta and inhale its smell. They detest water. They pluck their heads like sheep and smear their hands with ashes. They turn from living with their parents and families, leaving them to grieve. No rice balls are offered to the ancestors and funeral rites are neglected. No lamps are lit for them. They do not seek the refuge of the sixty-eight places of pilgrimage or feed Brahmins. They always remain filthy, day and night, and there is no tilak to be seen on their foreheads. They sit about in groups as if in mourning, and do not share in public activities. Brush in hand, begging bowl over the shoulder, they walk along in single file.

> From water came the jewels when Mount Meru churned the ocean. The gods established sixty-eight pilgrimage places where festivals are held and God is praised. The wise always walk. Muslims pray after ablutions, after bathing. Hindus worship. Water is poured on the living and dead to purify them.

> Nanak says, these pluck-haired devils will have none of this.

> Rain brings happiness. The cow can graze continually and the housewife churns the curds. With the ghee, havan, puja and festivals are sanctified.

> The Guru is the ocean, all his teachings are the rivers, bathing in them brings glory.

> If the pluck-haired do not bathe, says Nanak, let seven hands full of ashes be put on their heads. (AG 149-50)

A passage by Guru Amar Das reads:

> Some are Jains who wander in the wilderness. They are wasted away by the Primal Being. The Name is not on their lips and they do not bathe in places of pilgrimage. They pluck their heads with their hands, refusing to use a razor. Night and day they remain filthy. They have no time for social behaviour or responsibility. They live in vain.
>
> Their minds are soiled and impure. They eat one another's left overs. Without the Name and virtuous living, no one is ever blessed. By the Guru's grace the mortal merges in the One reality. (AG 1285)

One must say at the outset of discussing these passages that Jains would certainly deny their veracity and be concerned about what they would see as the pillorying of their beliefs and practices. Today, they are among the most respected communities in Indian society.

The criticism of Jains is in sharp contradiction to the portraits one is accustomed to of a benign, white-bearded old man. Though this picture may be as far from the truth as popular notions of the God of the Bible who has a long white beard and sits enthroned on a cloud! Why Guru Nanak made this attack is not the only perplexing matter. In fact, the question 'why' may be the easiest to answer.

Ishnan features strongly in Guru Nanak's teaching, together with Nam, meditation, and Dan, giving to the needy. Ishnan means 'washing' or 'bathing'. It seems a little strange for the emphasis to be upon an apparent ritual when this aspect of religious behaviour is so frequently under attack. Ishnan, however, for Sikhs, has to do with cleanliness and hygiene rather than ritual. Each morning most of the people of India, regardless of faith, bathe. This is often a preliminary to puja or, in the case of Sikhs, Nam simran, but it is a practice of which the Guru approved (the river Bein episode began with Guru Nanak bathing) and which he encouraged or even demanded of his disciples. At the other extreme come the Jains who, according to the Guru, rejoice in filth.

Jains are also non-theistic in practice. As we have noted the gods are beings who are themselves on the journey to enlightenment. Guru Nanak believed emphatically in one God who was essential to spiritual liberation. They were engaged in a vain journey. It is also asserted that Jains fail to give alms and reject their living families and their ancestors. They are clearly indifferent to society and lack community responsibility, 'Dan', the practice of almsgiving and mutual support, which Guru Nanak considered to be so important. In common with other groups, they denied the value of the householder life, which he saw as the cornerstone of society and the means by which men and women achieved spiritual liberation.

What is more difficult to comprehend is the Guru's apparent approval of Hindu practices which he elsewhere condemns, such as making pilgrimages or feeding Brahmins. Perhaps we may infer that he was not praising these activities but was really demonstrating how the Jains fell even below the expressions of Hindu devotion. There may be a chance that Hindus will experience God through the acts they undertake, the Jains have no hope, they are 'rejected by God'.

Plucking the hair on the head has drawn some comments from Sikhs who have seen in it an assertion that people should keep the natural form which they were given. This is a reason why Khalsa Sikhs and many others, though not all, keep the kesh intact, neither shaving nor cutting their hair.

One further consideration is the manner in which the Gurus regarded the self-torture practised by some austere Hindus. Sikhs have always considered the human body to be a temple of the Divine, infused by the jot. The extreme measures of Jain mendicants would seem to be a denial of this.

There are, however, a couple of lines in which Jains are treated more positively. Digambara is the name by which the group who went about naked are known. The Guru writes, with ahimsa in mind, the Jain tradition of not injuring sentient beings, or, to put it positively, reverence for life, a principle that greatly attracted Mahatma Gandhi:

> The naked Digambara is one who has compassion and examines his inner self. He slays his own self and does not slay others. You are but One, though your appearances are many. (AG 356)

This occurs in a passage where yogis, Jains and other practitioners of austerities are commended if the emphasis is placed upon trust in God.

Guru Arjan

In many respects Guru Arjan's influence upon the Panth has never been surpassed. It was arguably equivalent to that of the first and tenth Gurus. This is especially true of his significance when attitudes to other religions are discussed. He was ultimately responsible for its consolidation as an entity distinct from Hinduism and Islam. This he did principally by compiling a scripture, the Adi Granth. Like Hindus and Muslims the Sikhs now had a Book for which they claimed divine authority. The word adi means first in the cardinal sense of primal or primary. (Pehle is usually used of the first of a sequence). Adi Guru is a term frequently used to describe the original guru of a particular order. Caitanya as Adi Guru is revered even more highly than Krishna by his devotees.

The inclusion of the bhagat bani in the Adi Granth has already been noted. It is highly relevant to our examination of Sikh attitudes to other faiths for it is, perhaps, the only example of a corpus of literature not belonging to the particular religion being included in its scripture. (The inclusion of the Jewish scriptures in the Christian Bible is not comparable or relevant here.) It is an indication of the critical universalism of Sikh thought: critical in that only material that accorded with the Gurus' concepts of God and humanity was admitted. (An examination of all the writings of the bhakti poets, for example, will demonstrate that some passages were omitted and the suggestion is that this was because they did not comply with Sikh teachings.) It signified universalism by the inclusion of compositions by Hindus from a variety of varnas, and those of Muslims. Nothing already in the Qur'an, or *sruti* or smirti was incorporated and this might be considered significant. Synthesis or synchronism was evidently not in the fifth Guru's mind any more than it had been in Guru Nanak's. By including the works of the bhagats there may have been a suggestion that here was a scripture intended to be open to all. Certainly, present-day Sikhs make much of the bhagat bani as an example of ecumenical openness.

The scripture was installed in the Harimandir Sahib and here again openness is symbolised. Unlike a mandir, it had four entrances indicating that members of all four varnas might worship in it. By extension, in modern times it has become common to extend the symbolism to include people from the four corners of the earth. Sikhs also cherish a tradition that a Qadarite Sufi, Mian Mir, laid the foundation stone. Many modern Sikh historians question this, whilst acknowledging that he was probably present on the occasion.

Whether anything can be made of Guru Arjan's aspirations for his son, Hargobind, is a matter of conjecture. The name means 'world lord', and when the child was born, late in the Guru's life and that of his wife by Indian standards, he declared:

> The Sat Guru has sent the child. The long-lived child has been born by destiny. When he came and acquired an abode his mother's heart rejoiced greatly. The son, the saint of the world ruler lord [Gobind] is born. The primal writ has become manifest amongst all. In the tenth month by Divine Command, the baby has been born.

Sorrow has departed and great joy become manifest. The
Sikhs sing the gurbani in their joy. (AG 396)

Sikh confidence and self-esteem was high, as the above passage
demonstrates. The Panth was large enough and wealthy enough for
rivals to covet the gaddi. In part, Hargobind's birth was welcome as a
means of thwarting such ambitions. At this time the Mughal ruler
Akbar the Great was viewing all religions benignly. Jesuits were
present at his court and had some hopes of his conversion, while
Muslim courtiers and theologians were dismayed by his respectful
tolerance which extended to being married to a Hindu princess. Soon
after the Adi Granth had been compiled, enemies of the Guru told the
emperor that it contained material blasphemous to Islam. He asked to
see a copy and one was dispatched to him under the care of Bhai
Buddha and Bhai Gurdas. Portions were read, which Akbar approved
of, giving money towards the costs incurred in producing it, and
saying that he would visit the Guru on his return from Lahore. After
enjoying the Guru's hospitality, he acceded to his request that the
taxes of Punjab should be revoked for one year to offset the effects of a
serious famine. Non-Sikhs might conjecture that Guru Arjan hoped
that his might be the religion to provide the emperor with the alternative to Hinduism and Islam for which he was searching through his
monotheistic syncretism known as 'The Divine Faith'. This is not a
view found among Sikhs.

However, Guru Arjan also stated:

> I do not keep the fast [vrat] or observe Ramadan. I serve only
> the One who will save me in the end. The One World ruler is
> my God who ministers justice to both Hindus and Muslims. I
> do not go on hajj to the Ka'ba or worship at tiraths. My body
> and soul belong to the One and no other. I do not perform
> puja or namaaz. Taking the formless One in my mind I make
> obeisance there to God. I am neither a Hindu nor a Muslim.
> My body and soul belong to the One called Allah by Muslims
> and Ram by Hindus. (AG 1136)

Sikhs do not regard this as a denial of the authenticity of either of
the major religions but a proclamation of a God who transcends
them both.

Whatever Guru Arjan's hopes, they were dashed in only two years
after his meeting with Akbar. The emperor died and Guru Arjan was
accused of taking the side of the loser, Prince Khusrau, in the war of
succession won by Jehangir. The Guru was tortured and died in 1606,
becoming the first Sikh martyr. This event made the Panth reassess its

relationship with the Mughals and its self-understanding. There is a Sikh tradition that Guru Arjan told his son that when he mounted the gaddi of guruship he should wear two swords, those of miri and piri, signifying temporal and spiritual authority. The confidence that had been part of the Sikh psyche only a few years before was challenged and trust between the Panth and government never fully recovered.

Guru Tegh Bahadur and Guru Gobind Singh

1675 was the occasion of an even more devastating and significant event, the execution of the ninth Guru, the grandson of Guru Arjan. It is regarded by Sikhs unequivocally as an act of religious persecution. A group of Kashmiri pandits came to him looking for help against the aggressive attempts made by Emperor Aurangzeb to convert them. At the suggestion of his young son, he went to Delhi with a small group of followers where they were arrested. They were offered the choice of conversion or death. Preferring the latter they were executed, the Guru last. A gurdwara stands on the site in Chandi Chowk. The following are the words of Guru Gobind Singh, the son who had encouraged him to take up the Hindus' cause: 'For their frontal mark and their sacred thread he wrought a great deed in the age of Darkness. This he did for the sake of the pious, silently giving his head.'

From this time 'Mughal' is replaced by 'Muslim' in the vocabulary of persecution. But even now the story does not become one of unrelenting Sikh-Muslim hostility. In fact, Guru Gobind Singh was campaigning with Auranzeb's successor Bahadur Shah in 1708 when he received a mortal blow from an assassin. He exemplified the beliefs of his predecessors when he wrote: 'Salute him who is without the label of a religion.'

More fully, in a composition known as Akal Ustad, the tenth Guru wrote:

> Hindus and Muslims are one. The same Being is creator and nourisher of all. Recognise no distinction between them. Puja and namaaz are the same. All people are one, it is through error that they appear different. ...Allah and Abhek are the same, the Puranas and Qur'an are the same. They are all creations of the One.

The Eighteenth Century

Sikhs often present the century as a continuous armed struggle for survival when for much of the time, a price was put on the heads of

Sikhs. Paintings in gurdwaras often depict this graphically, the heads of decapitated Sikhs being carried on the heads of spears, and famous martyrs dying heroically. These undoubtedly still influence the attitudes of young Sikhs in the twenty-first century, but at the time lasting harm may not have been done to Sikh-Muslim relations, however, because of an event that took place at the very end of the period.

In the nineteenth century the Sikh Empire was established under Maharajah Ranjit Singh, who captured Lahore in 1799. It only came to an end as the result of two wars with the British after his death in 1839 and their annexation of Punjab in 1849. During this period Muslims served in the imperial administration and relationships generally seem to have been lastingly amicable. Elderly Sikhs, born as late as the 1930s, still talk of learning and speaking Urdu and of villages in which the religions existed harmoniously. Many Sikhs regard the Sikh Empire as a forerunner of the secular state established by Nehru in 1947.

It is significant that one of the reasons given by Sikhs for not participating in the Mutiny or First War of Independence in 1857 is that they had no desire to see a Mughal Empire restored as the result of success!

Independent India

Towards the end of the nineteenth century Sikhs were alarmed by the missionary zeal of two groups: Christian, and Hindu in the form of the Arya Samaj. The latter did not meet with great success because its founder, Dayananda Saraswati, displayed a scornful attitude towards Guru Nanak and Sikh scriptures. Sikhs perceived the danger posed by these sophisticated challenges and responded through the Singh Sabha movement which, from 1873, established educational institutions and generally encouraged learning. There was a flourishing of Sikh intellectual and cultural activity. Although one of the most important products of this resurgence was Bhai Kahan Singh Nabha's 'Hum Hindu Nahi' ('We are not Hindus'), as the twentieth century opened opposition became principally directed at the British Raj.

Partition and its Aftermath

In 1947 came the Partition of India. The Sikhs opted to live in secular India rather than join the Islamic state of Pakistan. Punjab was divided between the two. Lahore, the capital city of the nineteenth-century empire, became part of Pakistan, as did Guru Nanak's birth-place, Talwandi. This time there was outright warfare and although historians may distinguish between Mughal and Muslim in the seven-teenth and eighteenth-century conflicts, it was now a struggle between religions. Punjabi villages can still be seen in which the mosque has become a fodder store and mounds of earth show where Muslim inhabitants were buried after being killed. There is no need to pursue this topic further, other than to warn readers that they may encounter Sikh-Muslim hostility even though they have been told that Sikhs are friends with everyone. A few years ago, when an interfaith group planned a meeting on Sikhism, they were advised that no Muslims would attend but did not to take the comment seriously – came the day, no Muslims were in the audience. Nowadays the religions may enjoy better relationships in Diaspora communities, perhaps less so in India, and occasionally Pakistan which no longer has a Sikh popula-tion other than those caring for Sikh shrines – Sikh pilgrims to them have not always been welcomed with traditional hospitality, however, it should be stated that this has often been when India and Pakistan have been at war. At the time of writing Sikhs report well cared for gurdwaras and freedom of access.

Operation Blue Star 1984

Hindu-Sikh relationships have generally been good. There is a saying 'Hindu-Sikh bhai bhai', 'Hindus and Sikhs are brothers'. Sometimes part of a family will be Sikh while other members are Hindu. In the Diaspora it has become common to see Sikhs worshipping in a mandir especially where there is no local gurd-wara. They also share some celebrations, such as Diwali, and though they may interpret them differently, at the level of celebra-tion they may unite. During the events leading up to and after Operation Blue Star, in which the Indian army stormed the Darbar Sahib in 1984, there was considerable and often violent animosity between the two communities. Some of this has been consigned to history but the policy of militant Hindus, Hindutva, and other attempts to make India a more Hindu state perpetuate anxiety. No one should doubt how terrible and lastingly significant for the collective Sikh memory and the Panth's psyche this event was. Worldwide celebrations of the tercentenary of the Khalsa in 1999, including a major event at the Albert Hall and an exhibition at the Victoria and Albert Museum, which then travelled to other coun-tries, can disguise this. At the moment events are being planned to commemorate the compilation of the Adi Granth in 1604. To the extent that they will necessarily be associated with the Darbar Sahib they will rekindle pain, if not animosity and distrust. The fact that India now has a Sikh prime minister may have positive results.

The new Nanakshahi Calendar, which relates significant Sikh celebrations to the solar calendar instead of the Hindu Bikrami/Samvat era and begins with the birth of Guru Nanak, is not intended to distance Sikhs from Hindus (the principal melas will continue to be observed on the traditional occasions), but some people may regard it as a statement of Sikh distinction from Hinduism.

Sikhs actively participate in many inter-religious activities and, for example, have been present as observers at recent gatherings of the World Council of Churches. They do find it difficult, however, when they hear Jews, Christians and Muslims describing themselves as the 'three monotheistic religions'. By now, readers of this book should be aware that no religion can claim to be more monotheistic than that founded by Guru Nanak!

As for the future, one can only speculate, but it is clear that Sikhs will remain faithful to the critical universalism of the Gurus while the historical and social context in which they live is likely also to be influential.

An Explanation of Guru Nanak's Responses to the Forms of Religion He Encountered

From the above examples it seems impossible to provide a simple answer to the question of what Guru Nanak thought of the forms of religion he encountered. Certainly much that he saw met with his disapproval, but he could find a place for the Vedas and for Islamic practices and beliefs.

A clue to his views might be found in his attitudes to Jains and Naths. For these he had little time or none. The unimportance of God, which they seem to have preached by their conduct and their words, was in stark contradiction to a teacher whose message had God at its very heart.

His monotheism left no place for apparent polytheism. We know that a fundamental Hindu teaching is that God is one:

> Truth is One; sages call it by many names such as Indra, Mitra, Varuna, Yama, Garutman, or Matarishvan. (Rig Veda 1:164:46)

The Yajur Veda expresses the same truth as follows:

For an awakened soul, Indra, Varuna, Agni, Yama, Aditya, Chandra – all these names represent only One spiritual being. (32:1)

These words lie at the heart of the religion, but for many devotees and non-Hindu observers the reality seems to be polytheistic. The pictures and images which may be seen in a mandir, ranging from Rama and Hanuman, to Jesus, the Virgin Mary, Guru Nanak and Gandhi, might convey this message to the uninformed, rather than one of diversity within unity which is at the heart of Hinduism. Certainly, that seems to have been true of the village Hinduism that Guru Nanak experienced.

Duality, which popular, polytheistic Hinduism seemed to teach, was something else abhorrent to the Guru. Therefore rival religious systems would be inimical, not only the sectarian differences within Hinduism but also the discord which Islam might be creating in villages and regions that had once been Hindu. Social duality included caste and for its distinctions he again had nothing but disapproval. The equality of man and woman would also come under this heading.

An ethic, or lack of it, which did not emphasise social responsibility was also anathema. Thus the Jains were sharply rebuked, but again caste, which could express concern for members of one's own biradari but ignored others who were outside it, would be a target for his comments.

Finally, we are again left with the phrase Nam, Dan and Ishnan. At Kartarpur we may envisage a community focused upon these three principles of meditation upon the One, care for everyone regardless of gender, caste, wealth or beliefs, and cleanliness. To quote Bhai Gurdas, the great Sikh theologian who lived in the century after Guru Nanak:

The sun with its light dispels the darkness of night. Likewise the gurmukh, making people understand the importance of Nam, Dan, and Ishnan, sets them free from the bondage [of transmigration]. (Var 16, Pauri 7)

14

Who is a Sikh?

This would not have been a question that members of the community asked in the early days of the Panth. Had their relatives enquired, they might have received a reply of this nature:

> We are disciples of Guru Nanak and follow his teaching even more than his person. He teaches us that God lives within us, that outward religion is ineffective and likely to prove a distraction from the pursuit of true spirituality. Women and men may become his disciples [Sikhs], and people of all social groups and from all religious backgrounds are welcome.

Gradually these basics became embellished by such things as basing spirituality upon the Guru's hymns and lifestyle.

Bhai Gurdas may have been writing a century after Guru Nanak's death, but nevertheless his account of life at Kartarpur bears the hallmark of reality. It became the way of life for the Panth through the centuries and is still followed today.

> Discussions for the sake of knowledge and the melodies of unstruck sound were ever heard there. Sodar and Arti were sung and in the ambrosial hours Japji was recited. (Var 1, Pauri 38)

In Guru Nanak's own words:

> At amrit vela, the ambrosial hour before dawn, meditate on grace and greatness of the True Name. (AG 2)

and

> The Divine Essence is obtained in company of holy people [the sat sangat]. Fear of death disappears on meeting the Guru. One's destiny lies in meditating on Nam, through the Guru's Word, and finding God within oneself. (AG 598)

The ongoing aspirations of individual Sikhs, sangats and the Panth are summed up in these quotations.

Events encourage and may even require developments in the life of movements to take place. So Guru Amar Das summoned Sikhs when they might have been attending Hindu melas in order to make them to decide where their allegiance lay and to impose greater coherence upon a growing Panth. The most important change came about when, at Baisakhi 1699, the tenth Guru instituted the Khalsa. Not everyone became a member but the impact of the code of conduct resonated among the whole community, as it still does. Distinctive features, especially of appearance, became important, most notably the uncut hair and the turban, though it must be reiterated that not all men ever adopted these.

During the Mughal-Sikh and Afghani-Sikh struggles of the eighteenth century Sikhs were quite simply the enemy to be vanquished and destroyed whenever possible. Sikhs often declare that the purpose of keeping of keshas and wearing turbans was to protect Hindus who might otherwise have been mistaken for Sikhs. The victory of Maharajah Ranjit Singh ushered in a period of eclectic rule during which Sikhs enjoyed no distinctive favours and other communities were not disadvantaged. To external viewers the late nineteenth century was a time when the demise of Sikhism was likely. That it survived was largely the result of British respect for and eagerness to benefit from the warrior caste they held in high regard, as well as its own innate qualities. The army meant employment, secure service and a pension, but those who enlisted were required to keep the uncut hair and wear the turban.

During the nineteenth century gurdwaras had often passed into the ownership of Hindus. This had caused little concern as, frequently, Sikhism lacked any real distinctiveness. Hindu ceremonies conducted by Hindu priests were common. Late in the century Dayananda Saraswati and the Arya Samaj movement penetrated Punjab, winning some converts from Sikhism. Some ill-considered comments relating to Guru Nanak checked its progress. More important, however, was the success of Christian missionaries. In 1873 four Sikh students at the Amritsar Mission School declared their intention to convert. During the previous half-century, since 1834 when the American Ludhiana mission was established in Lahore, conversions had been few in number and mainly among lower-caste individuals and families. The threat to the Panth of educated members becoming Christians was not lost upon its own intelligentsia. On 1 October 1873 the Amritsar Singh Sabha was formed. The aims of these associations, which is what sabha means, were:

- to restore Sikhism to its original purity free from Hindu influences
- to publish books on Sikh history and religion;
- to establish newspapers and journals in Punjabi;

- to bring apostates back into the Panth;
- to interest the British in their educational programme and win their assistance in establishing Sikh educational institutions

The wisdom of the reformers in deciding that this was the policy most likely to achieve the desired success is clear. The liberating of Sikhism from Hindu influences of necessity required the reclaiming of gurdwaras from Hindu control, a matter that will be dealt with below. There was, however, also a need to provide a literary critique. One of the most important books to appear was *Hum hindu Nehi*, which translated means '[Sikhs] We Are Not Hindus'. This was written by one of the leading Sikh intellectuals, Bhai Kahan Singh Nabha, in 1898. In translation it begins 'Dear Khalsa ji'. The preface goes on to recall a story that Guru Gobind Singh told the Khalsa.

One day a donkey was going through a village when the Guru put the skin of a lion on it. People and other donkeys were terrified. It was able to wander at will taking food from stalls as it fancied. After a while it passed under a tree; one of the branches dislodged the lion skin and the donkey's owner realised how he had been duped. He began to beat the donkey mercilessly and once more burdened him with the pots that he had carried previously. The point of the story, the Guru said, was to make his followers recognise that it is not outward appearance only that makes a Sikh, it must be an inner transformation. If they continued to follow the distinctions of caste and other Hindu ways, or revert to them, they would no longer be Sikhs, any more than the donkey was a lion. Something of the point of this story may be discerned from a study of two important movements within the Panth in the nineteenth century. They represent movements that attempted to reform Sikhism before the Singh Sabha movement, and they have persisted to the present day. They are *Nirankari* Sikhs (not to be confused with Sant Nirankaris, followers of Avtar Singh, a person from a Sikh background but founder of an independent movement) and the *Namdharis*. This is probably the best place to discuss them. Each pertinently raises the question of Sikh identity, something that they helped preserve through their reform activities.

Nirankari Sikhs

The first Sikh reform movement preceded the annexation of Punjab by the British. In 1853 the annual report of the Lodiana (Ludhiana) Mission referred to a religious sect organisation which had already been in existence for eight or nine years 'but during the Sikh reign, fear kept them quiet'. It goes on to give this description of them:

They professedly reject idolatry and all reverence and respect for whatever is held sacred by Sikhs or Hindus except Nanak and his Granth. The Hindus complain that they even abuse the cow... They are called Nirankaris from their belief in God, as a spirit without physical form. The next great fundamental principle of their religion is that salvation is to be obtained by meditation on God. They regard Nanak as their saviour, in as much as he taught the way of salvation. Of their peculiar practices only two things are learnt. First, they assemble every morning for worship, which consists of bowing the head to the ground before the Granth, making offerings and in hearing the Granth read by one of their members, and explained also if their leader be present. Second, they do not burn their dead because that would assimilate them to the Hindus; nor bury them because that would make them too much like Christians and Musalmans, but throw them into the river. (*Punjab Past and Present*, April 1973, pp. 1-2)

Baba Dayal (1783–1854) was the founder of this movement, though he was born at Peshawar on the north-west frontier of Punjab and died at Rawalpindi. The enlightenment of Baba Dayal took place when he was only eighteen years old. One day when he was waving the chauri over the Guru Granth Sahib, he went into deep meditation and heard a voice saying:

Give up this ritualistic practice. You have been commissioned to expel the darkness of ignorance, superstition and falsehood from the minds of the people; illuminate their path by the true spiritual knowledge, propagate meditation of Nam-Nirankar ... You are a true Nirankari as you are a believer of God as spirit, without bodily form.

The slogan of his mission, which often provoked considerable opposition, was 'Jappo piario dhann Nirankar. Jo deh dhari sab khuar' ('All glory to the Formless One, God corporeal you must shun').

During the reign of Maharaja Ranjit Singh the Nirankari movement met strong opposition because it was perceived to be a threat to the religious harmony and tolerance which the ruler treasured. When Christian and Arya Samajist agitators entered Punjab it became popular, being seen as a parallel but indigenous agent of reformation. Many gurdwaras were purged of Hindu practices which had crept into their worship, but its main lasting contribution was to win acceptance for Anand marriage, the practice of being married in the presence of the Guru Granth Sahib to the singing of the Lavan of Guru Ram Das. At this time it was a common practice for weddings to be conducted by Hindu priests. Nirankaris are often called Nanak panthis because they reject the institution of the Khalsa, which they regard as an accretion introduced by the tenth Guru. Their headquarters was Dyal Sar near Peshawar. At partition in 1947 they lost access to it. Their headquarters is now at the Sri Nirankari Darbar in Chandigarh where the Nirankari Harimandir Sahib was opened in 1976. Precise numbers of members are not available, but it is estimated that in 1979 there were about 1,100 families in India some of whom are *keshdhari* and other *sahajdhari*.

Namdhari Sikhs

A second reform movement of this period still maintains its distinctiveness. This group is called the Namdharis, from the insistence which their most famous teacher Guru Ram Singh placed upon the practice of Nam simran. The name was introduced by Ram Singh himself, but Kuka (Shouter or Crier) is another name they have been given because their acts of worship often resulted in states of ecstasy in which they would dance and cry out (kuk in Punjabi). The movement came to prominence under their Guru Ram Singh (1816–84) He was as much a social reformer as a leader who, like Baba Dayal, wished to purge Sikhism of non-Sikh religious practices. Especially strong was his rejection of purdah, girl infanticide, child marriage, the sale of daughters into marriage, the giving of dowries, and the restriction of marriages to membership of the same zat. He supported the right of widows to remarry and the education of girls to the same standard as boys, especially in their knowledge of the scriptures. In his congregations men and women worshipped together. He encouraged the use of a white woollen mala in meditation and his male followers adopted a white sidhi pag, straight turban, laid flat across the front of the head. Guru Ram Singh also encouraged vegetarianism and forbade alcohol, smoking or drug taking.

Before 1849 when Punjab was annexed by the British they were already active in the state. In 1847 Sir Henry Lawrence, a wise administrator, issued the following proclamation on behalf of the Governor General of India:

> The priests [*sic*] of Amritsar having complained of annoyances, this is to make known to all concerned by order of the Governor General; British subjects are forbidden to enter the

Temple called Darbar at Amritsar with their shoes on. Kine are not to be killed at Amritsar, nor are the Sikhs to be molested or in any way to be interfered with.

A few years later a British order read:

No one should be allowed to interfere with the practice of his neighbour which that neighbour's religion permits.

This meant that Muslims could slaughter cows in Amritsar, which they then did.

The growing Kuka reform movement acquired a strong political dimension in this tense situation. At Vaisakhi on 14 April 1857, a month before the First War of Indian Independence broke out, the Namdhari flag was raised against the Raj. Guru Ram Singh's aims were:

- the boycott of government services;
- the boycott of educational institutions started by the British;
- the boycott of law courts established by the British;
- the boycott of foreign-made goods;
- the refusal to obey and readiness to resist laws and orders which are repugnant to conscience.

His swadeshi movement, that advocated the use of Indian-made products alone, and in particular cloth, alarmed the British who broke up a meeting of a large number of Namdharis in 1863 at Khote. Guru Ram Singh was inaugurating a series of Anand marriages but the British, misinformed by Brahmins who customarily conducted weddings, thought it was the beginning of a revolution to restore Sikh rule. The gathering was broken up and the Guru began his first period of internment at his headquarters in Bhaini Sahib.

In January 1871 an argument took place at Malerkotla between a Muslim butcher and a Sikh, Gurmukh Singh Namdhari. The Muslim judge who tried the case found against the Sikh and ordered an ox to be slaughtered in his presence. On 13 January some two hundred Namdharis marched on the town to avenge their comrade. Eight Kotla men were killed and seven Namdharis. The Namdhari survivors left the city and surrendered to the police. The Briton in charge of the state administration ordered their execution, without trial. On 17 January, forty-nine were executed by being blown to pieces in front of guns before which they stood voluntarily. The following day another nineteen died in the same way.

A group of Kukas also attacked and killed some butchers in Amritsar who had set up a slaughterhouse near the Lahori Gate. Some were killed and arrests were made. When Guru Ram Singh heard of the incident and that innocent people had been arrested he summoned the men to him and told them, 'Go to the court and confess your guilt so that the innocent may be saved.' This they did and were executed in September 1871. A third incident took place at Raikot in the Ludhiana district in July 1871, but the final act was the attack on a slaughterhouse at Maler Kotla on 15 January 1872 by about a hundred and twenty-five Namdharis. Many of them were arrested and sixty-five men were blown to pieces by canons. Although Guru Ram Singh was not implicated he was deported to Rangoon.

Unfortunately, the authority of the Akal Takht was used to denounce the Namdharis as non-Sikhs and thus, paradoxically, any opportunity to prevent the movement acquiring permanence was lost. Kukas were regarded as members of an illegal organisation until 1922 when they were recognised by the government in order to play them off against other Sikhs in the struggle for gurdwara control.

Namdharis had acquired several characteristics during this period. First, they had developed a consciousness of themselves as part of the Indian independence movement. The Maler Kotla Namdharis were the first large group of Indians to be executed by the British after 1857 and the British had exiled their leader. Second, their theory of guruship is such that they believe in the kind of authority which existed from the time of Guru Arjan and certainly the period of Guru Gobind Singh when a living Guru existed as well as the scripture. Third, as has been noted, they emphasise the social, educational, and economic concern of Sikhism. Fourth, they attach great importance to spiritual and moral development and observance.

Namdharis do not believe that Guru Gobind Singh died at Nander; instead he became a recluse. Eventually he installed a man named Balak Singh as Guru and in 1841 Ram Singh came under his influence and was made twelfth Guru by him. Kukas believe that Guru Ram Singh, who was imprisoned in Rangoon, still lives and will one day reappear. Meanwhile, first his brother, Hari Singh, then his nephew, Partap Singh, became vice-regent Guru from 1906 to 1959. In 1959 his son, the present Guru, Jagjit Singh, was installed as leader of the movement. Guru Ram Singh was a Ramgarhia and it is among this social group, though not exclusively, that many Namdharis are to be found.

Their spirituality, heritage and beliefs, emphasis on amrit initiation, and ties of kinship keep them within the Sikh community. However, they do not accept the sole authority of the Guru Granth Sahib, and they believe in a living Guru who, though he is happy to be described as the 'vice-regent' of Guru Ram Singh, is nevertheless the spiritual head of something like 700,000 followers. They have their own marriage rites, which include circling around a fire (havan) while Lavan is read. Of all Sikh groups, they look to the return of a Guru, Guru Ram Singh, who, they believe, will inaugurate an era of world peace.

At Ardas Namdharis add the sentence: 'Bless us with the sight of your name, Guru Ram Singh, may the glory of your name increase, and may the whole world be blessed by your name', to the concluding words used by other Sikhs.

Namdhari Sikhs take spiritual and moral guidance from the Adi Granth, the Dasam Granth, and the teachings of Guru Ram Singh.

★ ★ ★

There can be no doubting that these two movements, infrequently mentioned in books by Sikhs, played a significant part in preserving and reforming the Panth. Whenever their Sikh credentials are questioned, usually on the grounds that they have living Gurus and do not subscribe to the unique authority of the scripture, they are defended by Sikhs who realise the debt that is owed to them. Nirankari influence was primarily aimed at the purification of the Panth, whereas the Namdharis anticipated the swadeshi policy of Mahatma Gandhi by over fifty years, and the Quit India movement by nearly three-quarters of a century.

The Shiromani Gurdwara Parbhandak Committee

Sikhs founded the political Chief Khalsa Diwan in 1902, to 'cultivate loyalty to the crown', but a grassroots movement was developing which would jeopardise this loyalty. The First World War pushed the struggle into the background, but in 1920 a proclamation was made from the Akal Takht, Amritsar, that a committee was to be set up to manage all Sikh shrines. This was known as the Shiromani Gurdwara Parbandhak Committee (Central Gurdwara Management Committee), usually referred to by its initials SGPC. Sikhs organised themselves into a volunteer brigade, the Akali Dal (army of immortals), dedicated to wrestling gurdwaras from their custodians (mahants). The recruitment of nihangs, men dressed in blue, heavily armed and sworn to defend gurdwaras to the death, increased. A class of men who had been left over from the eighteenth century once more assumed relevance. There were clashes with the army. The Akali Dal was declared illegal but in 1925 the Sikh Gurdwaras Act was passed.

This listed the gurdwaras and placed them under the control of the SGPC. For the first time in panthic history an attempt was made to answer the question, 'Who is a Sikh'. A Sikh was defined as 'one who believes in the Gurus and the Guru Granth Sahib and is not a patit (apostate)'. It asserted:

> Sikh means a person who professes the Sikh religion, or in the case of a deceased person, who professed the Sikh religion or was known to be a Sikh during his lifetime. If any question arises as to whether any living person is a Sikh, he shall be deemed respectively to be or not be a Sikh according as he makes, or refuses to make, in such a manner as the State Government may prescribe, the following declaration: 'I solemnly declare that I am a Sikh, that I believe in the Guru Granth Sahib, that I believe in the Ten Gurus, and have no other religion.'

The reference to one who was a Sikh but is now dead may relate to land ownership. The purpose of the Act was to bring gurdwaras under Sikh control. The rights of Hindu families to gurdwara property would cause controversy. There is nothing in the declaration that Nirankari or Namdhari Sikhs might find embarrassing though they may sometimes demur at the term 'Guru Granth Sahib'. Most intriguing and significant is the phrase, 'and have no other religion'. To understand this rare assertion of Sikh exclusiveness it is necessary to remember the historical and social circumstances. There was still a need to emphasise Sikh distinctiveness. 'We are not Hindus' was a statement not universally appreciated. Many Hindus claimed that Sikhs were just turbaned Hindus, and do even to this day. The conservative, right-wing Hindutva movement seeks to win them to join in a common cause against such non-Indian religions as Islam and Christianity. Sikhs have not usually been affected by the requirement that they should have no other religion, at least as far as can be observed from glimpses of village life and even Diaspora gurdwaras. Hindu families are known to bring up one of their sons as a Sikh. For a Sikh to marry a Hindu of the same zat is far more preferable than for the partner to be a Sikh from another zat. Sikhs were quick to establish gurdwaras in towns where they settled throughout the world because congregational worship is essential to them in a way that it may not be to Hindus. Nevertheless, in those rare places where Hindus met for puja and there was no similar Sikh arrangement, Sikhs were to be found worshipping with Hindus. Hindus in similar circumstances often worshipped in gurdwaras.

The Delhi Gurdwara Act of 1971 that gave control of Delhi's gurdwaras to the Delhi SGPC was modelled to some considerable extent on that of 1925. Its definition of a Sikh is, however, more precise and adds a new element that had become more important during the intervening half-century. It reads:

> Sikh means a person who professes the Sikh religion, believes and follows the teachings of Sri Guru Granth Sahib and the ten Gurus only, and keeps unshorn hair. For the purposes of the Act if any one poses the question whether a living person is a Sikh or not, he shall be deemed respectively to be a Sikh according as he makes or refuses to make in the manner prescribed by the rules, the following declaration: 'I solemnly affirm that I am a Keshdhari Sikh, that I believe in and follow the teachings of the Guru Granth Sahib and the Ten Gurus only, and that I have no other religion.'

The significant additions are the inclusion of the word 'only' after 'Ten Gurus'; this can certainly be considered to be aimed at Namdhari Sikhs. The term 'Keshdhari Sikh' is also restrictive. A Keshdhari Sikh is one who keeps the hair uncut and, in the case of men (and some women), wears a turban. He is at least distinctively Sikh although he has not taken amrit.

The declaration excludes Sikhs who are known as sahajdhari. These are members of the Panth who cut their hair and do not have beards. The actual meaning of the term is uncertain: 'slow adopters' was used by scholars of the Singh Sabha movement, suggesting that they were on their way to taking amrit but, for some reason, held back. This is not a satisfactory explanation, however; sahajdharis are not Khalsa members in the making. The term may derive from the word sahaj, meaning the ineffable bliss experienced by the devotee in the union with God that is the climax of Nam simran. Other Sikhs are prone to use it in a derogatory manner. Even more pejorative is the word mona. This should apply to a Sikh who has undergone a ritual shaving of the head, but it is commonly used to describe someone who has cut his/her hair. Debate centres upon the place of sahajdharis within the Panth. Gurdwaras generally allow them to vote in elections for the committee, but they are often denied the right to stand as candidates.

An *amritdhari* Sikh is one who has taken amrit and is a Khalsa member, subject to its code of discipline as laid down in the Rahit Maryada. Such a person is regarded as the ideal to which the rest of the Panth should aspire.

The proportion of Sikhs who fall into each of these categories is difficult to assess. No official records exist listing amritdharis, and sahajdharis cannot be distinguished by their appearance from non-Sikhs. National censuses do not tend to differentiate but to invite people to opt for the religious movement of their choosing, if any.

Sants

The word sant may be used to refer to people like Kabir who were members of the late medieval bhakti tradition. Sant-sipahi is used to refer to the ideal Sikh, humble and pious, devoted to Nam, willing to be the dust under everyone's feet, yet also possessing the qualities of a soldier (sipahi), being honourable and loyal in the defence of justice. Here, however, it is being used in the specific sense of a Sikh spiritual teacher. With the notable exceptions of the Sikh Nirankaris and Namdharis, after 1708 no one in the Panth would use the term guru or allow it to be used of them. From time to time spiritual teachers emerged who attracted a following. These men are known as sants. There are many of them. Their devotees may be closely attached to them or may only visit them occasionally when they have a reason, perhaps a domestic crisis. Sants often live in a dera, a compound consisting of the family house, outbuildings and, possibly a gurdwara. They are unlikely to proclaim themselves to be sants but they will have built up a reputation for spirituality that eventually leads to them having many followers. Perhaps here it should be said that to draw parallels with Hindu gurus should be resisted. A sant should point beyond himself to the principles of Sikhism.

Sometimes the movement outlives its original teacher and a successor may be chosen by him or by leading members of the group. It may flourish internationally either because its members migrate or because the sant himself feels led to take his message overseas. The teaching or *sampradaya* can be completely in accord with Khalsa orthodoxy and orthopraxy, or it may emphasis some particular facet. For example, there may be one sant group that preaches the importance of amrit and holds regular ceremonies of initiation. Another might stress the value of akhand paths and may perform them almost continually. Vegetarianism may be an important principle, and strong objections to the use of tobacco and alcohol are almost the norm among sant groups. Women devotees may wear turbans as well as men, and a group may emphasise a distinctive colour, perhaps black, whereas normally this is unimportant. Membership may be open to anyone, but there can be a tendency to follow a sant who is of one's own zat.

Organisation is very much in the hands of the sant and those to whom responsibility has been delegated by him. Sant gurdwaras are likely to have nominated rather than elected committees. A sant may spend much time travelling from his headquarters to other parts of the world where his devotees live. When he makes a visit, he may stay in specially prepared rooms in the gurdwara or with a family. As many followers as are able will take leave from their work to minister to his needs. The owner of a taxi firm, for example, may put his cab at the sant's disposal, however long his stay. Most gatherings will probably take place in the evening, the rest of the day being given over to other activities, such as visiting, planning, and discussing organisational matters, though the sant's decision will always be final. Obedience is the hallmark of a devotee's response to his or her sant. His hukam, command, is to be accepted without question. Some sants exercise considerable political influence, for example, Harchand Singh Longowal who was assassinated in 1985 for attempting to achieve an accord with Prime Minister Rajiv Gandhi.

Sikh identity can be influenced considerably by the teachings of the sant that one may follow. In this respect it is necessary to examine one such group. In 1971 Harbhajan Singh Khalsa Yogiji founded the Sikh Dharma of the Western World in the USA. It now has several thousand members and claims to have members in almost twenty countries. In fact the most recent website information gives the number as 10,000 with 139 ashrams in the USA, 4 in Canada, and 86 in other countries. The highest concentration is on the west coast of America. Yogi Bhajan, to give the sant his popular name, went to the USA in 1969 and began to teach kundalini yoga. Some of his students showed an interest in the total lifestyle of his Sikh faith, which included vegetarianism, the rejection of drugs, of sex outside marriage, and the acceptance of a world-view that emphasised equality and service. Daily Nam simran was at the heart of his teaching. A number of young people requested that they might take amrit. Upon initiation they each took the name Khalsa and dressed in white from head to foot, both men and women wearing turbans. They have shown themselves to be devout Sikhs, sometimes even exceeding the standards of other members of the Khalsa. Many of them have learned Punjabi and can read and write gurmukhi. Their children are now growing up in the faith.

The presence of these Gora (white) Sikhs has caused some questioning among the rest of the Panth. Can they be true Sikhs if they are not Punjabi? They belong to no zat, unless they constitute one of their own. Izzat, family honour and pride, is unknown to them and unappreciated by them. Sikhs whose antecedents come from Punjab are often reluctant to marry with them; in fact most marriages seem to be within the movement. This group raises acutely the question of how Sikhism can exist cut off from its Punjabi roots. Yogi is now an old man. There is some discussion about its future once he has left the scene. On the other hand, there are many mature members capable of leading it into the future. It is an aspect of Sikhism to be watched carefully.

The power of caste proved too strong for Hindu reform movements to find a place for the lowest members of society with much success. Two of these turned hopefully to Sikhism and somewhere around the beginning of the twentieth century converted in large numbers. They were chamars and Shudras, cobblers and sweepers, both carriers of ritual pollution by birth and employment. Each dealt with the skins of animals and similar detritus. Here the names by which they came to be known within the Panth and religions in north India will be used.

Ravidasis

Ravidasis are people who belong to the same social group as the mystic Ravidas (c.1414–c.1526), that is cobblers, chamars, ritually impure men and women. They tried to improve their untouchable status by becoming Sikhs who were considered to be egalitarian and had included compositions of Ravidas in their scriptures. The attempt was not successful, anymore than the effort which some made to improve their lot through conversion to Christianity. They were permitted to participate in the religious life of the Panth but usually not to serve on committees, and Sikhs of other social groups would not intermarry with them. They have responded, especially since Partition, by establishing their own religious institutions, although they keep the Sikh outward form and use the Guru Granth Sahib as the focus of their worship, giving priority to the bani of Ravidas. Many of them retain the turban and uncut hair and have been mistaken for Sikhs by researchers and social workers. Often they now prefer to call their place of worship a sabha (association) rather than gurdwara. An edition of the works of Ravidas is being prepared which may replace the Guru Granth Sahib in worship. Sikhs describe him as a bhagat or sant, his followers call him Guru.

Balmikis

Equally unfortunate is the story of the Shudra (sweeper/cleaner caste) experience. This untouchable group, whose remaining Sikh members are known as Mazhabi Sikhs, found its attempt to gain full acceptance within the Panth equally difficult. It has therefore turned from Sikhism and Christianity to Balmiki (sometimes written as Valmiki), the legendary author of the great Hindu epic, the Ramayana, and tutor of Rama and his brothers. They recognise him, a Shudra sage, as their founder guru and have installed the Ramayana as the focus of their worship, sometimes side-by-side with the Guru Granth Sahib. However, they tend no longer to keep the uncut hair and turban and seem closer now to Hinduism than Sikhism, though they would insist, like the Ravidasis, on their distinctiveness but also on their wish to remain in good standing with Sikhs as well as other religious groups. Like the Ravidasis, their meeting places tend to be called sabhas rather than gurdwaras. A Shudra named Bhai Jaita Ranghreta recovered the head of Guru Tegh Bahadur in Delhi and brought it to the martyr's son, the tenth Guru. For this his family and caste were honoured. The Guru told him, 'Ranghretas are the Guru's own sons'. Pictures of this episode are often to be found in Balmiki sabhas, but their very existence bears witness to the reality that the esteem in which the Guru held them is not shared today by the Sikh Panth generally.

From what has been written in this section it will be clear that the question of Sikh identity cannot be answered easily or as satisfactorily as some students of religion might wish. There are hints or guidelines, the Gurdwaras Act and the Delhi Gurdwaras Act being most significant, but when elections for the SGPC are called arguments quickly arise concerning those who have the right to vote. The same is true with regard to elections for local gurdwaras. The decisions relating to candidature are much clearer. The requirement is usually that a person should be keshdhari. But what might happen should the SGPC become a committee with worldwide authority, as some desire? How would it settle the issue of identity, especially if its members were elected on a worldwide basis? Yogi Bhajan has been honoured by the SGPC in the past. Would one of his Gora Sikhs be welcomed as a member?

Sikh identity is very much a matter for Sikhs to discuss and decide, if they so wish. To outsiders, westerners in particular, who may be used to clear definitions and credal statements, the issue can be frustrating, but there is no reason why the Panth or any other movement should define itself for the benefit of outsiders. The strength of Sikhism lies in the fact that it is not hierarchical and lacks ecclesiastic authorities to which all members defer. Though having said this, it is not for want of trying that the SGPC lacks ultimate and universally acknowledged authority. Towards the end of the last century, for example, it passed a decree that langar should be taken seated on the floor. In most Diaspora gurdwaras the practice of eating at tables had become accepted. Some gurdwaras immediately conformed. Other sangats argued that were Guru Nanak living in Vancouver today, he would eat at table since no one there sits on the ground as they do in India. The argument continues with some Sikhs arguing that the SGPC is a political body rather than a religious one, and that it lacks the right to legislate on such issues.

The discussion is ongoing. It might come to a head if, for example, a national legislative body wishes to include Sikhs as representatives. Probably, for that purpose, keshdhari Sikhs might be appointed or elected, but this would not necessarily affect the reality that the majority of Sikhs may well be sahajdhari!

There are a number of centres of spiritual authority of importance in regulating the life of the Panth. These are known as takhts and proved necessary when the period of the Gurus had ended and matters of orthopraxy, and sometimes orthodoxy, needed to be decided.

Takhts

The word literally means thrones. They are seats of temporal authority and are five in number.

Akal Takht, Amritsar, was established by Guru Hargobind on a site opposite the focus of spiritual authority, the Harimandir Sahib. In the eighteenth century the Sarbat Khalsa, the entire body of the Khalsa, met in front of it to make important decisions, such as that of uniting against Afghan invaders. The Akal Takht was built by Guru Hargobind as his seat of temporal authority and for these historic reasons it is the pre-eminent centre of authority. It is the place from which decisions affecting the whole Panth should be pronounced.

Patna Sahib, Bihar, where Guru Gobind Singh was born.

Keshgarh, Anandpur, where the first amrit ceremony was held.

Nander, near Hyderabad, where Guru Gobind Singh died.

Damdama Sahib, near Batinda. This was only declared to be a takht in 1966. Guru Gobind Singh spent some time there during which he completed the final recension of the Guru Granth Sahib.

Jathedars

The term jathedar originally referred to the leader of a group of Sikh volunteers, a jatha, usually soldiers, who gave themselves to the full-time service of the Panth. 'Captain' might be an English equivalent. Now it is used of the head of one of the five Sikh takhts. He is a paid official chosen by the SGPC to serve for an indefinite period. He (no woman has yet been appointed) may issue hukam namas, decisions binding on the Panth, but should only do so after a panthic conference. This rule is not always observed, so a Jathedar can find himself in conflict with the SGPC and may be dismissed for exceeding his authority or using it wrongly in its view. These tensions detract from the authority of both.

The purpose of jathedars and takhts is not clearly defined. The jathedars sometimes assume political roles and occasionally make doctrinal statements which should be pronounced by the whole Panth gathered in the presence of the Guru Granth Sahib. Such a gathering, a sarbat khalsa, is not practicable, especially when twenty million Sikhs live in so many countries.

Where authority lies in Sikhism is a difficult question to answer as anyone knows who has tried to involve Sikhs in meetings of religious leaders. In practice, it is in the Guru Granth Sahib and the accepted guidance of the Rahit Maryada. At local level it lies in the sangat or those chosen to lead it or speak for it.

15

Sikhism and the Twenty-First Century

Migration

In 2003 the most expensive gurdwara in the world was opened in Southall, England. The cost is estimated at £13 million, but a figure of £24 million has also been mentioned. The 1951 census gave only 330 members of the local population as being born in new Commonwealth countries. Ten years later this had risen to 2,540. In 2001 the number of Sikhs in Ealing was 25,625, of which Southall is a part, and in neighbouring Hounslow 18,265. (2001 is the first census since 1851 where a question on religious adherence has been asked.) Sikhs first met in a hall, hired on Sundays, for Diwan, a copy of the Guru Granth Sahib being taken from a private house. Some forty or fifty people attended the gathering for worship. In 1961 a house was purchased and two rooms were converted for use as a gurdwara. In 1967 a dairy was bought and converted into a gurdwara. In 1975 it was expanded when the next door building was obtained. Ten years later the land on which the new gurdwara now stands was bought in Park Avenue, but the foundation stone was not laid until 1999. The purpose-built gurdwara is centrally heated, has an underground car park and another for disabled persons. The latter are taken by lift to the main hall. Special attention has been given to their needs, possibly for the first time in the history of gurdwara construction. The langar hall accommodates two thousand people. There are also rooms for wedding receptions and for use as classrooms to meet the needs of extensive educational programmes. The palki sahibs, one gold and one silver, were constructed in India and shipped to England. The story of this new gurdwara is an expression of the maturation and confidence of Sikhs in one particular part of the Diaspora. It can be mirrored in many other countries.

Migration among Sikhs is not a new or even recent phenomenon. As Guru Nanak journeyed around India and beyond, he visited established communities that had originated in his own region. Khatri merchants were particularly active. The tenth Guru was born in Patna Sahib, over a thousand miles from Punjab. One might say that a characteristic of the Sikh is that he is a migrant.

It was not until the last decade of the nineteenth century, however, that Indians, including Sikhs, began to migrate in appreciable numbers. The British were opening up East Africa. They could provide the educated and trained men who would run the region while the native Africans would do the menial tasks, but the men needed in the middle were missing, those who could organise and oversee the workforce. Sikhs from Punjab, mostly Ramgarhias, met the requirement. They and their families stayed until African independence followed by an Africanisation programme that rendered their presence unnecessary or undesirable. Not all, however, left such countries as Kenya in the 1960s. Some are still to be found there, but a fairly typical story that one may hear is of a Sikh air traffic controller at an airport training the African whom he knew would replace him. Ugandan Asians, many of them Sikhs, were unceremoniously deported. India was a foreign country to them. The UK became their destination of choice because they had been working with the British for three-quarters of a century and were familiar with their ways.

Meanwhile, other Sikhs migrated, often influenced by the Partition of India in 1947. Some had moved from what became Pakistan to find no land and little work in the new India. Others were finding that there were few prospects for the younger members of Jat agrarian families. Some highly educated and well-qualified Sikhs discovered that businesses or the state could not afford to employ them.

The example with which this chapter began is only one of many that could have been selected. It describes the growth of a community from insignificance to one in which Asians form a considerable proportion of the population. The usual story is of a few men migrating to a place where they had hope of employment, being followed by other male relatives whom they helped to find work, and later by wives and children. Southall is near to Heathrow airport, which was expanding at the time. Hence its attraction. Sikhs did not go to coal-mining areas, which were closed to non-family members and also did not constitute an expanding labour market. The British scene was often one of highly educated men having no choice but to take blue-collar jobs. Now the situation has changed radically; Sikhs are to be found holding posts in universities and businesses, many of which they themselves own.

In terms of religious practice Southall is fairly typical, renting, purchasing and then purpose-built premises being the natural growth as the community expanded. The lavishness of the new Southall gurdwara may not be the aspiration of every sangat, but all share a wish that their place of worship should be worthy of their Gurus and scripture.

Other areas, such as North America, attracted well-qualified Sikhs who were needed by the newly developing high-tech industries. The story of each country and even each community deserves independent scrutiny. Whereas generalisations might be made fifty years ago, they are now recognised not to be valid.

Sikhs are to be found worldwide but most of them, the exception being Gora Sikhs, originated in Punjab where they may still have ties. The next section relates to this dispersal of Sikhs as well as indicating that the main centre of population is still northern India. What can be stated with certainty is that Sikhs have emigrated principally to the English-speaking countries and those that were formerly part of the British Empire, for reasons to do with culture and language.

Sikh Population

The number of Sikhs worldwide can only be estimated. Several websites provide information, but figures vary widely from about 23 million to 39 million. Much depends on the method of computation used. The total Indian population in 2001 is given as 1,027,015,247. Religious statistics are yet to be provided. Two per cent is a popular proportion given to Sikhs, hence about 20.5 million. It is obvious that Sikhs are to be found in greater numbers in some areas than others, for example, Punjab, Haryana and Delhi. If Punjab has a population of 24.28 million and 85% are Sikhs, that will give them a total of 20.64 million in the state. If Delhi's population is 13.78 million and 10% are Sikhs, that will give a further 1.38 million. Whether the estimates of 85% and 10% respectively for Punjab and Delhi are accurate will not be known for some years. Meanwhile, estimates should be treated with caution, bearing in mind that all groups are more inclined to favour higher estimates than depress their numbers.

In the countries of the Diaspora there is similar uncertainty, especially regarding the USA. Some estimates give 1 million for the whole of North America, others for the United States alone. More reliable is the census total of 2001 for Canada, 147,000; for Australia, 12,000 in 1996; for New Zealand, 2,800 in 2001; and for the UK, 336,000. Malaysia has about 57,000 and Singapore 20,000. Latin America is said to have 9,000 and Europe excluding the UK a further 130,000, which seems overlarge though there are many gurdwaras in continental Europe; again those interested are encouraged to consult the web. African numbers are very uncertain. We are left with the inclination to accept 23 million as the total of Sikhs worldwide.

Changes in lifestyle

In the chapter on the gurdwara and worship it was suggested that religious life has become more highly organised in Diaspora areas. Punjabi is still, and will remain, the most important language in the gurdwara. Sometimes the local vernacular language is used for notices and discussion, be it Danish or English, but the lingua franca is Punjabi. Classes are regularly held so that young Sikhs may acquire their mother tongue as it continues to be called. Some gurdwaras are introducing more and more of the language of their new home into worship.

The myth of return has still some potency. This is the hope that is frequently prevalent among migrants that one day they will go back to the land of their birth to end their days, whether it be the Welsh in Patagonia or Sikhs in the Diaspora. Sometimes the aspiration is achieved, but more often the fact that the children are settled in the new country, have married and provided their parents with grand-children means that it remains a dream rather than a reality. This does not prevent an abiding attachment to the ancestral village resulting in large sums of money being sent home, to improve the family property or build a new gurdwara. It can now be difficult to find places of worship that are over fifty years old. So-called historic gurdwaras have been replaced by modern buildings all of a similar architectural type. One may regret the practice but cannot complain. It is what the nineteenth-century neo-Gothic revival did to churches in England!

The future of the Diaspora seems assured. The possible conflict between science and religion that may trouble Jews, Christians, and Muslims has no place among Sikhs. Western-style secularism is more of a potential challenge as values based on the Guru Granth Sahib, upheld by the Panth, are seen to be less attractive than materialism. Many Sikhs, however, can steer a path between the two.

There are sometimes clashes between Sikh tradition as preached and endorsed in Punjab and the Diaspora. The Guru Granth Sahib will always be installed and read in the Gurmukhi version, but that leaves plenty of scope for the language spoken daily by sangat members. The charge sometimes put that Sikhism is being replaced by Punjabiism cannot be sustained, though the emphasis upon the language issue may encourage the outsider to make this observation. The langar issue mentioned earlier also invites questions about the home country's readiness to accept diversity.

Panthic organisation is likely to become an important issue in the twenty-first century. If the SGPC and the system of Takhts is to carry weight and influence, reform will be necessary. Other religions are having to respond to what might be called democratic demands, Sikhism is unlikely to escape the challenge, especially when the Panth is fundamentally democratic in its theocracy and has never been hierarchical since the times of the Gurus. Even then, as a number of stories from the life of Guru Gobind Singh show, the Guru could and did bow to the will of the Panth. In our speculation we are in danger of speedily moving beyond Sikhism as it is to a vision of what it might become. This, hopefully, is excusable to some degree when we are aware that it is a dynamic way of life capable of wide appeal and potentially extremely resilient; it is not an institution.

Appendix
Passages of Importance to the Panth

These are many in number and include the Rahit Maryada, Guru Nanak's Japji, and the other banis that Sikhs meditate on daily. There is no room to include them all here but the two that follow are chosen because sooner rather than later anyone who becomes interested in Sikhism will encounter them. Both are used on public occasions. Although the first is a mantra, it is not intended to be secret, though it is formally taught to Sikhs about to be initiated into the Khalsa community.

Mul Mantra/Mantar

Of all Guru Nanak's many succinct statements, the Mul Mantra must rank among the best examples. It sums up his teachings about the nature of God and was considered of such fundamental importance that Guru Arjan not only placed it at the beginning of the scripture which he compiled in 1604, he also put it at the head of each of the musical ragas into which he divided the bani. It stands almost as an introduction to the more important compositions. The term is translated by Professor Shackle as 'root formula'. It is the nearest that Sikhism comes to having a credal statement. It is used on such occasions as moving to a new house or setting up business premises and is taught to initiates about to be admitted to the community of the Khalsa. Tradition suggests that it was Guru Nanak's first utterance when he emerged from his experience of being taken to the Divine Court. When the phrase Mul Mantra was first used by the Guru or the Panth is also uncertain, but Guru Nanak does use it in his bani where he makes the following affirmation:

> Uttering the Mul Mantra and Hari Nam, the elixir of eternal life, I have attained the Perfect One. (AG 1040; Hari, one of the Hindu names for God, is frequently used by the Guru.)

This quotation clearly indicates that the phrase Mul Mantra was first used by Guru Nanak himself. In addition to his use of the phrase, the respect that the Panth had for him makes it unlikely that anyone else would have arrogated to himself the right to name the verse.

Bhai Gurdas equates the word Oankar with God. In one verse he says: 'In one bang Oankar created and spread myriads of forms' (Var 18, Pauri 1). Elsewhere, he writes: 'Oankar, transforming into forms, created air, water, and fire. Then separating earth and sky, he threw two flames of sun and moon in between them' (Var 4, Pauri 1). Of even more direct relevance to a reference to the Mul Mantra is Var 6, Pauri 19. It reads:

> That the True Guru [Sat Guru] is Truth incarnate and the basis of meditation is well known [to the gurmukh]. Satinamu, Karata Purukh is accepted as the basic formula, the Mul Mantra by the gurmukh.

In this passage Bhai Gurdas quotes the phrase Mul Mantra and cites some of the words which are included in it. Furthermore, he indicates that it is the basis for meditation. By the time of Guru Arjan, the use of the Mantra was clearly well established.

We are now in a position to examine the Mul Mantra, which is also transliterated as 'Mantar'. It reads:

Ik oankar sati namu karata purukhu nirbhau nirvairu akal murit ajuni saibhang gurprasad. (AG 1)

It can be rendered in English as follows, though students will come across many other translations:

There is One Being [God]; Truth by Name; Immanent in all things; Sustainer of all things; Immanent in Creation; without fear and hatred; not subject to time; Formless; Beyond Birth and Death; Self-revealing; known by the Guru's grace.

In the section below passages from the Guru's writings will not be quoted extensively. Many verses relating to the concepts are already to be found in the sections on Sikh teachings. In discussing the Mul Mantra generally, one must realise that it reflects upon a Hindu world-view.

Ik Oankar

Ik, One, is the all-important affirmation that begins the Mantra. The symbolic representation of this phrase is found on the canopy over the Guru Granth Sahib in gurdwaras. Its location is reminiscent of that of

੧ ੳ ਸਤਿਨਾਮੁ ਕਰਤਾ ਪੁਰਖੁ
ਨਿਰਭਉ ਨਿਰਵੈਰੁ ਅਕਾਲ ਮੂਰਤਿ
ਅਜੂਨੀ ਸੈਭੰ ਗੁਰ ਪ੍ਰਸਾਦਿ ॥
॥ ਜਪੁ ॥
ਆਦਿ ਸਚੁ ਜੁਗਾਦਿ ਸਚੁ ॥
ਹੈ ਭੀ ਸਚੁ ਨਾਨਕ ਹੋਸੀ ਭੀ ਸਚੁ ॥੧॥
ਸੋਚੈ ਸੋਚਿ ਨ ਹੋਵਈ ਜੇ ਸੋਚੀ ਲਖ
ਵਾਰ ॥ ਚੁਪੈ ਚੁਪ ਨ ਹੋਵਈ
ਜੇ ਲਾਇ ਰਹਾ ਲਿਵ ਤਾਰ ॥ ਭੁਖਿਆ
ਭੁਖ ਨ ਉਤਰੀ ਜੇ ਬੰਨਾ ਪੁਰੀਆ ਭਾਰ ॥
ਸਹਸ ਸਿਆਣਪਾ ਲਖ ਹੋਹਿ
ਤ ਇਕ ਨ ਚਲੈ ਨਾਲਿ ॥

Mul Mantra and the opening lines of the Japji of Guru Nanak.

Om in a Hindu mandir. Like Om, Ik Oankar represents a belief in one fundamental reality. In fact it is made up of the numeral One (Ik) and the letter 'O' which stands for Om of which Oankar is a cognate, though many Sikhs emphasise its distinctiveness, arguing that they are not the same word. The Katha Upanishad says of Om:

> That which the Vedas declare, that which all austerities utter, that in desire of which men become students, that word I tell you briefly is Om. That Word is even Brahman, the Supreme. (2:15)

The implication of the Isa Upanishad is that the whole universe is Om.

Oankar is, however, the term preferred to Om by Guru Nanak. It is made more emphatic of the uniqueness of God by the inclusion of Ik. The use of a number in this way is distinctive to Sikhism, if not unique. No one using the Mul mantra can possibly doubt Guru Nanak's monotheism. He wrote:

> The One, Oankar, created Brahma. The One fashioned the human mind. From the One came mountains and ages. The One created the Vedas. (AG 929)

The One is beyond comprehension and may only be experienced, not described:

> O mother, the attributes of God cannot be comprehended. Without actually seeing [experiencing] one cannot say anything about God. How is the One to be described, O mother? (AG 1256)

In many of his compositions the Guru states his vision of God and the vibrancy of creation. For example: 'In the three worlds is your light [joti] and I realise that you permeate them' (AG 352). But he felt the need to sum up his concept of God in an easily remembered mantra. It is not an attempt to present a crippling definition of God – his own spiritual experience taught him how impossible this would be.

There was a need to witness to or state the distinctiveness of the God he was proclaiming. The Mul Mantra might be understood in the context of a community of women and men most of whom came from a Hindu background. Though they would have joined the Panth as individuals, they would still belong to and live in extended families whose culture was Hindu. At a popular level Hinduism conveys the impression of being polytheistic though at its essence it is mono-theistic or monist. Therefore, Guru Nanak begins by affirming the oneness of deity.

Sati Namu

Guru Nanak uses a variety of names to describe God, some drawn from Hinduism, others from Islam. He seems content to use these, however each has some sectarian connotation. Even Allah, which comes from the Arabic al-ilah which means 'the God', might call to mind purdah or Babur's invasion of Punjab, and Krishna might not evoke ideas from the Bhagavad Gita but popular erotic myths. Here perhaps a parallel may be drawn with the Christian use of 'Father' when speaking of God. For children and young people whose experience is of a parent who is an uncaring absentee or an abuser, 'Father' is not a word that signifies love, affection or trust. Satinamu, on the other hand, places emphasis on God who is free from cultural or personal significance. Nam is so full of meaning in the hymns of the Guru, and Sat, Truth, is a concept capable of infinite expansion. Both Truth and Nam are limitless. Of course, it would be wrong to pretend that Satinamu cannot be incarcerated in beliefs and associations like those relating to other names for God which have grown up over the intervening centuries.

Karta Purukh

The creative Being. The One who is experienced through Nam simran as Truth is also the creative spirit who pervades the universe, which has no independent existence of its own. God is, therefore, immanent. This word is not included in the Mantra but is implied because the very nature of Being is presence within creation. A key basis of Guru Nanak's teaching is that the Being of God is present within each human being. Were it not so the whole promise of liberation would be futile. The statement also affirms the teaching that God is a continually active creator.

Nirbhau and Nirvair

Interpretations of God as omnipotent but tyrannical are almost universal among religions at a popular level at least. Guru Nanak's God is devoid of fear (nirbhau) and enmity (nirvair). These should also be characteristics of the gurmukh. As Guru Arjan in the Sukhmani, the hymn of peace, says:

> He cuts his fetters and becomes free from enmity [nirvair] and night and day adores the Guru's feet. (AG 292)

> The person who meditates on the fearless God [nirbhau], has all his fears dispelled. By God's grace the mortal is liberated. (AG 293)

Akal Murit

God is not subject to time and is formless. This 'Being beyond time', which is one of the interpretations offered for the word 'Akal', is to be contrasted with popular images of God which teach about a divinity who walks the earth. Anthropomorphism of this kind and beliefs in gods who become incarnate is completely alien to the Guru's awareness of God and doctrinally anathema to Sikhs.

Ajuni

This is understood to be a reference to the rejection of the concept of avatar, but it is also linked with Akal and Sati. Again many traditions, at a popular level, suggest that gods become incarnate. The God of the Mul Mantra is beyond time, eternal.

Saibhang

This eternal Being is also self-existent and self-sustaining. Mantras, rituals, prayers, austerities cannot induce, even less compel action. On the contrary, as Karata Purukh implies, God is already and ceaselessly active.

Gurprasad

The earlier phrases of the Mul Mantra focus on the nature and being of God. This final phrase declares that God is gracious but grace must always have an object. One cannot be gracious to oneself! The One who is Beyond Time, who is present in creation, which itself is the product of Akal Purukh, is manifest to humanity through grace and not as the result of searching, of ritual practices, or of yogic asceticism. The initiative lies with a God who wishes to reveal it. It may also be found, though only through the grace of the Guru, in the Guru's Word (Gurshabad) and in women and men who are gurmukh. Guru Nanak taught that the true believer should share in the Guru's blessings and in the privilege and responsibility of declaring them to those as yet unaware and unenlightened.

Ardas

The practice of meditation, Nam simran, is so important in Sikhism, and so much part of the Indian religious tradition, that it is easy to overlook the fact that prayer is also an essential part of Sikh worship. The purpose of this section is therefore to act as a reminder and to provide an explanation and English version of the prayer that is used wherever the sangat gathers in worship or for other ceremonies, for example, marriages and funerals. It should also be made daily by every Sikh, especially at the end of morning and evening recitations of the prescribed bani.

The word for prayer is ardas. Its ultimate origin is the Sanskrit root 'ard', to ask or beg; its more immediate source was the Persian 'arzdasht', a petition or address made by an inferior to a superior. At the time when the prayer is offered by the sangat, the whole congregation stands as a sign of respect and humility with palms pressed together in the eastern manner, facing the enthroned Guru Granth Sahib. A member of the congregation, man or woman and of any social status, comes forward to offer the prayer on behalf of the sangat. Guru Amar Das said:

> The Almighty is the one who knows, who acts, and does what
> is right. So stand before God and make your supplications.
> (AG 1093)

It is not easy to describe the atmosphere as Ardas is being offered. To an observer it seems to be the most sacred part of the service, a few minutes in which past and present and geographical distance become insignificant. The sangat stands in the presence of God, as it did when the Gurus led prayer, and it feels itself surrounded by the sangat here and in eternity, though it must be noted that it does not confine its concern to Sikhs who have worshipped and served God.

The prayer is in three parts. First, Sikhs are told to remember God and the Gurus in the words taken from the Dasam Granth. Particular mention is made of the boy Guru, Har Krishan, who compensated for his father's sorrow at the inadequacy of Ram Rai and who, though a child, was seen to possess the spirit of guruship by those who visited him in Delhi. During his brief stay there he became known as a healer. The portion attributed to Guru Gobind Singh ends with words of respect for his father Guru Tegh Bahadur. The 'nine treasures' is a phrase frequently used in Hindu writings to describe spiritual and material prosperity.

The congregation is then told to keep the Guru Granth Sahib, the repository of God's word, in mind as being the manifest form of God. They are then instructed to remember the faithfulness of other devout Sikhs. The 'beloved five' are the first Khalsa members who were prepared to give their lives to the Guru. The tenth Guru's four sons died in the struggle against tyranny, as did many others, particularly the forty Sikhs who deserted him at Anandpur but later changed their minds. As they were returning to the Guru they encountered a Mughal force. They fought with it until the last Sikh was struck down. Later, the Guru came to the place and found one Sikh alive. The dying soldier asked for forgiveness which the Guru immediately gave and the place, Khidrana, was renamed Muktsar, the place of deliverance. This part of the prayer also remembers many other martyrs of Sikhism and certainly keeps alive the memory of persecution in commending loyalty. The 'seats of authority' are the seats of doctrinal authority held by the granthis of the Akal Takht, Amritsar; Keshgarh Sahib, Anandpur; Patna Sahib gurdwara, Bihar; Hazur Sahib at Nander, near Hyderabad; and Damdama Sahib at Talwandi Sabo.

The final section of Ardas is supplicatory and God is asked to keep the Khalsa faithful, to bless the whole of mankind and heed individual petitions. Particular items may be added to this part of the prayer. The sangat may remember its sick or bereaved, members preparing to travel overseas, for example, or a newly married couple if Ardas is being offered at a wedding service. The local community might also be brought before God, the city council or local interfaith group, and also non-Sikhs known to the Panth who are ill or have suffered bereavement or some family joy.

The prayer begins with invocation before proceeding to supplication. It reads as follows:

Ardas

Victory to the Supreme Being.

May almighty God protect us.

First remember almighty God, then call to mind Guru Nanak, Guru Angad, Guru Amar Das, Guru Ram Das; may they help us. Remember Gurus Arjan, Hargobind, Har Rai, and Guru Har Krishan whose sight removes all sorrows. May we remember Guru Tegh Bahadur at whose invocation the nine treasures come hastening to our home. May they help and protect us at all times. May we always enjoy the protection of the tenth Guru, Guru Gobind Singh. May he always be with us.

Disciples [Sikhs] of the Guru meditate on the Guru Granth Sahib, the visible form of the Guru. Repeat the name of God.

Waheguru!

Think of the glorious deeds of the five beloved ones [panj piare], the Guru's four sons, the forty saved ones, and others who were steadfast and long-suffering. Remember them and call on God.

Waheguru!

Call to mind those who kept the Name in their hearts and shared their earnings with others.

Waheguru!

Those who allowed themselves to be cut limb from limb, had their scalps scraped off, were broken on the wheel, were sawn or flayed alive, remember them.

Waheguru!

Think of those who cleansed the gurdwaras, permitted themselves to be beaten, imprisoned, shot, maimed, or burned alive with neither resistance nor complaint, and call on God.

Waheguru!

As you remember the seats of authority and other places touched by God's feet, call on God.

Waheguru!

May the Khalsa remember the Wonderful Being, and as it does may it be blessed.

May God's protection be on all members of the Khalsa wherever they may be. May God's glory be proclaimed and God's way prevail.

May victory attend our charity and our arms. Let us trust in divine grace.

May the Khalsa always be victorious.

May the Sikh choirs, flags and mansions remain forever.

May the kingdom of justice come.

May Sikhs be united in love and humility, but exalted in the wisdom of remembering God. O Khalsa, say the Supreme Being is wonderful.

Waheguru!

O true King and loving Father, we have sung your sweet hymns, heard your Word which gives life and talked of your many blessings. May these find a place in our hearts so that our souls may be drawn towards you.

O Father, save us from lust, anger, greed, worldly attachment and pride: keep us always attached to your feet.

Grant your Sikhs the gift of discipleship, the gift of your Name, the gift of faith, the gift of discernment, the gift of reading your Word with understanding.

O kind and loving Father, through your mercy we have passed our days in peace and happiness: grant that we may be obedient to your will.

Give us light and understanding so that we may please you.

We offer this prayer in your presence, wonderful One.

Forgive us our wrong acts, help us to remain pure.

Bring us into the good company of those who love you and remember your Name.

Through Nanak may the glory of your Name increase and may the whole world be blessed by your grace.

Waheguru ji ka Khalsa, Waheguru ji ki fateh!

Bibliography

This is a select bibliography intended to help readers extend their knowledge of Sikhism. Most of the books listed include detailed bibliographies, though not always with annotations.

Surveys of Sikhism

W. Owen Cole and Piara Singh Sambhi, *The Sikhs, Their Religious beliefs and Practices*, Sussex Academic Press 1995. A study of all aspects of the religion but with the emphasis upon the religious and spiritual areas.

Hew McLeod, *Sikhism*, Viking Press 1997. Professor McLeod has been the most important contributor in the area of Sikh studies during the last twenty-five years. He is an historian by training and aptitude and the great strength of this book is in that direction.

Historical Surveys

J. S. Grewal, *The New Cambridge History of India: The Sikhs of the Punjab*, Cambridge 1990. A thorough, scholarly account of the Panth in its historical context from its beginnings until the consequences of Operation Blue Star in 1984.

Gopal Singh, *A History of the Sikh People*, World Book Centre, second edition, 1988. One-time ambassador to Bulgaria and Goa who lived close to the major events of the twentieth century.

Harbans Singh, *The Heritage of the Sikhs*, Manohar 1994 edition. This has proved a popular study since 1984 when it was first published. The author was one of the leading scholars of his generation.

Khushwant Singh, *A History of the Sikhs*, (2 vols) Oxford 1977. His study ends at 1974; a pity because he too has lived at the heart of Sikh history throughout his long life.

Mohinder Singh, *The Akali Movement*, National Institute for Punjab Studies 1997. An examination of events influencing the development of the Panth in the early twentieth century.

The Guru Period

M. A. Macauliffe, *The Sikh Religion*, Oxford 1909; reprinted 3 vols., 1985. This survey has seldom, if ever, been out of print. It provides a traditional story of the ten Gurus and the bhagats and a translation of many of their writings. It was written before the length of printed copies of the Guru Granth Sahib was fixed at 1,430 pages so the Raga references are provided.

W. H. McLeod, *Guru Nanak and the Sikh Religion*, Oxford 1968. An attempt to distinguish between the Guru of history and the Guru of faith which met with a similar response to that given to studies referred to in Schweitzer's *Quest of the Historical Jesus*. Valuable in itself, but enhanced by an excellent analysis of his teachings.

The B40 Janam Sakhi, translated and annotated by W. H. McLeod, Guru Nanak University, Amritsar 1980. A convenient provision of an opportunity to read one of the traditional biographies of Guru Nanak much cherished and used by Sikhs.

The Scriptures

Charanjit K. AjitSingh, *The Wisdom of Sikhism*, One World Publications, Oxford 2001. A very attractive anthology that takes the reader to the heart of Sikh spirituality and devotion, compiled by one of Britain's leading Sikhs.

Nikky-Guninder Kaur Singh, *The Name of my Beloved*, HarperCollins 1996. This volume in the Sacred Literature Trust series contains passages used in daily devotion and other important materials such as the marriage hymn, Lavan, and Ardas.

W. H. McLeod, *Textual Sources for the Study of Sikhism*, Chicago 1990. Major scriptural passages are augmented by selections from important texts in Sikh history.

Jodh Singh and Dharam Singh, *Sri Dasam Granth Sahib*, text and English translation (2 vols), Heritage Publications, Patiala 1999. As the authors affirm, this is the first complete rendering of the entire corpus in English.

Manmohan Singh, *Sri Guru Granth Sahib*, English and Punjabi translation, SGPC Amritsar 1964. The gurmukhi text is accompanied by modern Punjabi and English translations. The eight-volume work can often be obtained from gurdwaras.

Pashaura Singh, *The Guru Granth Sahib: Canon, Meaning and Authority*, Oxford 2000. Analysis of the text is accompanied by essays on such important matters as the Raga organisation of the Adi Granth, Guru Arjan's editorial perspective, and the Word as Guru.

Pashaura Singh, *The Bhagats of the Guru Granth Sahib*, Oxford 2003. A thorough examination of one of the most important aspects of the Sikh scripture: the inclusion of material by non-Sikhs.

Ethics

Avtar Singh, *Ethics of the Sikhs*, Punjabi University, Patiala 1970.

Nrpinder Singh, *The Sikh Moral Tradition*, Manohar, Delhi 1990.

These publications set out the classical statements on Sikh ethics. As yet no one seems to have given the same amount of thought to contemporary moral issues. Perhaps Sikhs in the Diaspora will address these in the near future. Members of the Sikh Diaspora group sometimes discuss them on the web.

The Diaspora

The Sikh Diaspora; N. Gerald Barrier and Verne A. Dusenbury (eds.), Chanakya Publications, Delhi 1989. Indispensable for a study of the early period of migration and the reasons for it, but since it was written a third generation of Diaspora Sikhs has been born. This is the kind of issue that requires constant updating.

Joseph T. O'Connell, Milton Israel, Willard G. Oxtoby, W. H. McLeod, J. S. Grewal (eds.), *Sikh History and Religion in the Twentieth Century*, University of Toronto 1988. A collection of essays covering a broad sweep of important cultural and historical issues.

Encyclopaedias

W. Owen Cole and Piara Singh Sambhi, *A Popular Dictionary of Sikhism*, Curzon/Riverdale Press 1990.

W. H. McLeod, *Historical Dictionary of Sikhism*, Scarecrow Press 1995.

The Encyclopaedia of Sikhism: Harbans Singh (ed.), 4 vols., Punjabi University, Patiala 1995. Long-awaited and many years in preparation, partly because of the editor's meticulous care. An indispensable tool.

Other important books

Kerry Brown (ed.), *Sikh Art and Literature*, Routledge 1999. An illuminating examination of Sikh literature, mysticism and art. Complements the volume edited by Susan Stronge..

M. Juergensmeyer, *Religion as Social Vision*, California 1982. Especially relevant to a study of the Ravidasi and Valmiki groups and their relation to the Panth.

W. H. McLeod, *Sikhs of the Khalsa: A History of the Khalsa Rahit*, Oxford 2003. An indispensable study of the Khalsa throughout its four hundred-year history.

Jodh Singh and Dharam Singh, *Varan Bhai Gurdas: Text and Translation*, 2 vols., Heritage Books, Patiala 1999. The first complete translation of the writings of the Panth's first theologian apart from the Gurus.

Parm Bakshish Singh Devinder Kumar Verma, R. K. Ghai and Gursharn Singh (eds.), *The Golden Temple*, Punjabi University, Patiala 1999. This anthology covers most of the subjects relevant to the Darbar Sahib and its history.

Patwant Singh, *The Golden Temple*, E T Press, Hong Kong 1989. A beautifully produced book which might dangerously be described as 'coffee table'. It is far more than that being an excellent guide to Sikhism's major shrine.

Susan Stronge (ed.), *The Arts of the Sikh Kingdoms*, Victoria and Albert Museum 1999. Though specially written to accompany the memorable exhibition that marked the Khalsa tercentenary, it has permanent importance for students of Sikh culture and history.

Websites

Users of the Internet will know that sites come and go with alarming frequency. It is, however, possible to find a number of sources for Sikhism itself and for Namdhari Sikhs, Nirankari Sikhs, Ravidasis and Valmikis, as well as Sant Nirankaris who are completely separate from Sikhism.

Glossary

adi — first, original

Adi Granth — Sikh scripture compiled under the direction of Guru Arjan in 1604 (abbreviated here as AG)

ahimsa — reverence for life: non-violence

AG — see Adi Granth

akal — Timeless, a term used to describe God. Sometimes as Akal Purukh used as a name of God

Akal Purukh — The Timeless Being or Being beyond Time; also referred to as parmeshwara/parmeshar, the Ultimate being, God

Akal Takht — Central seat of temporal authority in Darbar Sahib

akhand path — a continuous reading of the Guru Granth Sahib taking forty-eight hours. Associated with occasions of great sorrow or joy and a means of observing Sikh festivals (gurpurbs)

amrit — nectar or elixir of immortality in Guru Nanak's writings

amritdhari — Sikh who has been initiated into the Khalsa, taken amrit

amrit pahul — Sikh initiation rite, also known as amrit sanskar or khande ka pahul

amrit vela — literally, the ambrosial hour, before dawn

anahad shabad — the unstruck sound or music, articulated in Om and the Vedas, and the Guru Granth Sahib

anand — bliss, a quality or attribute of God. Believer's state of equipoise

Ardas — an important Sikh prayer used at the conclusion of an act of worship and at most ceremonies

Arti — Hindu worship using lighted lamps. Part of the Sikh hymn Sohila

bani — speech, hymn. Confined to the compositions found in the Sikh scriptures

Bedi — clan (got) of Guru Nanak, belonging to the Khatri caste (zat)

bhagat — a devotee or exponent of bhakti. Used as a general term for the Hindus and Muslims whose compositions are included in the Guru Granth Sahib, the Bhagat bani

bhai — brother, normally used to describe men respected in the community

bhakti — loving devotion to a personal God; Bhakti marga, the path of devotion

chardhi kala — high spirits; cheerfulness

chauri — yak hair, nylon, or peacock feather fan waved over the Guru Granth Sahib.

chela — the disciple of a guru, used as a synonym for Sikh

darshan — view, vision; sight of a holy person or one of importance such as a ruler

das — slave, often suffix to name of a devotee of God, e.g. Tulsi Das, Ram Das, Nanak Das

Dasam Granth — collection of writings attributed to the tenth Guru and made by Bhai Mani Singh twenty or thirty years after the Guru's death

dharamsala — commonly in India the term means a hostel or inn. In the early Sikh period it was used to describe the place where Sikhs assembled for worship. Later superseded by the word gurdwara

Diwali — a major Hindu festival falling at the beginning of the light part of the month Kartik, October/November

diwan — royal court, name given to a Sikh act of worship

diwan hall — room where worship takes place

gaddi — seat or throne of a guru

gosht — a discourse

got — exogamous group within a zat

granth — collection, book

Guru Granth Sahib — Sikh scripture, earlier known as Adi Granth

granthi — one who looks after the Guru Granth Sahib (and reads it in worship)

grihasthi/gristhi — householder; second stage of Hindu life, the one which Guru Nanak taught subsumed all others

gurbani — Guru's teaching; the content of the Guru Granth Sahib

gurdwara — literally the door of the Guru, consequently a building in which the scriptures are kept and used in worship. It may be purpose built or a room in a house.

gurmat — teachings of the Guru. Sikh theology

gurmukh — literally from the Guru's mouth. One who follows the Guru

gurmukhi — the script in which the Guru Granth Sahib and Punjabi is written.

gurpurb — anniversary of the birth or death of a Guru, usually observed by an akhand path

Guru — commonly explained by Sikhs as meaning gu = darkness and ru = light. One who delivers devotees from ignorance to enlightenment

Gurshabad — Guru's word, Sikh scripture

haumai — self, self-reliance, a word which sums up the nature of natural, unenlightened humanity

hukam — order, command (used in Qur'an, sura 18.26)

Janam Sakhi — a traditional biography, literally birth evidences or life evidences; religious biographies

janeu — sacred thread worn by high-caste Hindus

Jap — repetition of the name of God or of a mantra composition by Guru

Gobind Singh

jap mala — a circle made of 108 strung beads of sandal wood or some similar seeds, or of knotted cotton used in meditation or repeating the name of God, simran

Japji, Jap Sahib — the most famous of Guru Nanak's compositions

Jat — a farming caste (zat) dominant in the Punjab

jati — endogamous caste group, Punjabi zat

jiva — soul inner self (cf. jot)

jivan mukti — liberation whilst still in the flesh; the jivan mukt is a liberated person

jot — indwelling divine light

Kal Yug — the fourth, last and present cosmic age or kalpa, literally related to Kaliyug, the losing throw at dice. It lasts 320,000 years: it is characterised by the deficiency of dharma. Bhakti marga, the path of devotion is the main form of worship. The present age is the Kal Yug.

karah parshad/ prashad — the gift of God to devotees prepared in an iron bowl (karah). It is shared at Sikh gatherings to express equality and membership of the Sikh family.

Kartarpur — The key place where the original Sikh community was set up by Guru Nanak.

keshdhari — literally one who wears the hair uncut

Khalsa — the Pure Ones. The community or family of initiated Sikhs

khande ka amrit — Sikh form of initiation introduced by Guru Gobind, also known as khande ka pahul

Khatri — mercantile caste (zat) to which the Sikh Gurus belonged

Khuda — one of the names used by Muslims for God – the Holy, al-Quddus

kirpan — the sword worn by initiated Sikhs

kirtan — singing of songs in praise of God normally to the accompaniment of musical instruments

langar — free kitchen instituted by Guru Nanak, and emphasised by the third Guru

mahant — head of a Hindu religious institution or monastery – used of those who controlled gurdwaras before the Gurdwaras Act of 1925

maharaja — title given to an Indian ruler

mala — string circle of woollen cords, or beads of 108 knots, sometimes called a seli or jap mala used in Nam simran

man — mind

manji — 1. small string bed (charpoy); seat of Guru Granth Sahib; 2. Men and women appointed by Guru Amar Das to preach and teach the practice of Nam simran.

manmukh — one who follows the guidance of his own mind rather than that of God

mantra — word or verse often believed to confer power and insight; given by a Guru to a disciple at initiation

maya — the natural world, created by God and therefore real but capable of distracting from God-centredness

mela — festival

miri — signifying temporal authority

mukti — spiritual liberation (Punjabi); also moksha (Sanskrit)

mul — basic

nadar — divine grace

Nagar kirtan — (usually) gurpurb procession when the Guru Granth Sahib is processed through the streets led by men representing the panj piare and followed by many of the Sikh community

Nam — literally name, implies the power of the name of God; also Sach Nam, the True Name

Nam japna — repetition of God's name

Nam simran — meditation upon God's name, Nam

Nirankari — worshipper of God as the Formless One

nirguna — unconditioned, without qualities

nitnem — daily 'prayer book' containing important shabads

pandit — Hindu teacher of traditional vedic learning

Panth — literally path; used to describe the Sikh and other communities

patit — lapsed Sikh

pauri — stanza (literally 'staircase') of a hymn ascending to a climax of praise

piri — spiritual authority; from pir, Muslim, Sufi, religious leader or teacher

pothi — a book

prasad — gift received by devotee at worship

puja — Hindu worship

Puranas — eighteen books containing the mythology of Hindus

Qur'an — the scripture of Islam

raga — musical form

ragi — singer of ragas in the Sikh community, sometimes semi-professional

Rahit Maryada — Code of Discipline which all Sikhs initiated into the Khalsa must observe

Rama — incarnation of Vishnu, hero of the great Hindu epic, the Ramayana

saguna — with form or qualities, used of God

sahaj — ultimate state of mystical union

sahajdhari — observant Sikh who does not keep the outward form, especially the uncut hair

sampradaya — school, sect, tradition

sangat — gathering, congregation

sant — (1) popularly a synonym for sadhu; (2) the north Indian tradition to which men like Kabir belonged; (3) a Sikh spiritual teacher

sarovar — pool

Sat Guru — the True Guru, God

sewa/seva — service on behalf of humanity or the community, not confined to caring for Sikhs

shabad — word, hymn or song, cf. bani

Shiromani Gurdwara Parbandhak Committee — elected committee responsible to the Indian government for Gurdwara Sikh affairs in the Punjab and Haryana (SGPC)

sikh — disciple

simran — meditation

shlok — couplet

Sohila — group of hymns forming the Evening Prayer of Sikhs

sruti — that which has been heard, revealed scripture, the Vedas

Sufi — a Muslim mystic

Takht — seat of temporal authority; see also Akal Takht

tirath — a place of pilgrimage

udasi — (1) order of ascetics claiming Shri Chand, son of Guru Nanak as their founder; (2) preaching journey of Guru Nanak

Vahiguru/Waheguru — Wonderful One. A popular name for God. Literally, 'Praise to the Guru'. According to one tradition represented by Bhai Gurdas, formed from the initial letters V (Vishnu), A (Allah), H (Hari), but more probably a compound word made from vah (praise) and guru.

Vaisakhi/Baisakhi — a major Sikh festival, anniversary of creation of the Khalsa, and beginning of spring harvest in Punjab

var — ode, eulogy, ballad, epic poem

varna — the four-fold division of Hindu society

varnashramdharma — Hindu code of conduct laid down in the Dharma Shastras to be followed by Hindus of the first three social divisions

Vishnu — major Hindu deity, regarded as the ultimate expression of God by many devotees

yoga — 'union'. A technique leading to a state of liberation through the union of the human spirit with Ultimate Reality

zat — endogamous caste grouping (Hindi jati)

Index